www.wadsworth.com

www.wadsworth.com is the World Wide Web site for
Thomson Wadsworth and is your direct source to dozens
of online resources.

At *www.wadsworth.com* you can find out about
supplements, demonstration software, and student
resources. You can also send e-mail to many of our
authors and preview new publications and exciting new
technologies.

www.wadsworth.com
Changing the way the world learns®

A Precious Liquid

Drinking Water and Culture in the Valley of Mexico

Michael C. Ennis-McMillan
Skidmore College

Case Studies on Contemporary Social Issues:
John A. Young, Series Editor

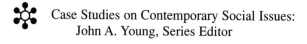

Australia • Brazil • Canada • Mexico • Singapore
Spain • United Kingdom • United States

A Precious Liquid: Drinking Water and Culture in the Valley of Mexico
Michael C. Ennis-McMillan

Senior Acquisitions Editor: *Lin Marshall*
Assistant Editor: *Leata Holloway*
Technology Project Manager: *Dee Dee Zobian*
Marketing Manager: *Lori Grebe Cook*
Marketing Assistant: *Teresa Jessen*
Marketing Communications Manager: *Linda Yip*
Project Manager, Editorial Production: *Christine Sosa*
Creative Director: *Rob Hugel*
Executive Art Director: *Maria Epes*
Print Buyer: *Rebecca Cross*
Permissions Editor: *Audrey Pettengill*

Production Service: *Sara Dovre Wudali, Buuji, Inc.*
Copy Editor: *Heather McElwain*
Cover Designer: *Rob Hugel*
Cover Image: *Michael C. Ennis-McMillan*
Cover Printer: *Courier Corporation/Stoughton*
Compositor: *Interactive Composition Corporation*
Printer: *Courier Corporation/Stoughton*

The logo for the Contemporary Social Issues series is based on the image of a social group interacting around a central axis, referring both back to a tribal circle and forward to a technological society's network.

All photos are reprinted with the permission of the author except where noted.

© 2006 Thomson Wadsworth, a part of The Thomson Corporation. Thomson, the Star logo, and Wadsworth are trademarks used herein under license.

ALL RIGHTS RESERVED. No part of this work covered by the copyright hereon may be reproduced or used in any form or by any means—graphic, electronic, or mechanical, including photocopying, recording, taping, web distribution, information storage and retrieval systems, or in any other manner—without the written permission of the publisher.

Printed in the United States of America
2   3   4   5   6   7   09   08   07   06

Thomson Higher Education
10 Davis Drive
Belmont, CA 94002-3098
USA

The map on page xviii, "Mexico," is from the HOUGHTON MIFFLIN EDUCATION PLACE® web site (http://www.eduplace.com/ss/maps/pdf/mexico.pdf). Copyright © Houghton Mifflin Company. Reprinted by permission of Houghton Mifflin Company. All rights reserved. The map may be printed and copied for classroom use. Any other use of the material is strictly prohibited unless written permission is obtained from Houghton Mifflin Company.

Chapter 6 is adapted from *OPPOSING CURRENTS: The Politics of Water and Gender in Latin America,* ed. Vivienne Bennett, Sonia Davila-Poblete, and Maria Nieves Rico, pp. 137–153, Pittsburgh, PA: University of Pittsburgh Press.

Chapter 7 is from *Medical Anthropology Quarterly* (15(3): 368–390, 2001).

For more information about our products, contact us at:
Thomson Learning Academic Resource Center
1-800-423-0563

For permission to use material from this text or product, submit a request online at
http://www.thomsonrights.com.
Any additional questions about permissions can be submitted by
e-mail to **thomsonrights@thomson.com.**

Library of Congress Control Number: 2005935300

ISBN: 0-534-61285-7

To my mother, Bunny Ennis, and my friend and colleague, Jill D. Sweet. I am deeply grateful for your love, support, and good humor while I engage in my anthropological pursuits.

Contents

List of Figures and Tables

FIGURES

TABLES

Foreword

ABOUT THE SERIES

These case studies feature the work of anthropologists who address contemporary issues affecting everyday life. Each case study examines an issue of socially recognized importance in a geographical, historical, and cultural context—and provides a comparative analysis highlighting its global connections and implications. The authors write absorbing narratives that include descriptions of how they apply their skills and carry out their responsibilities in the communities and organizations they study. Their engagement with people goes beyond mere observation and research, as they illustrate from personal experience how their work has implications for advocacy, community action, and policy formation. They demonstrate how anthropological investigations can build our knowledge of human society and at the same time contribute to achieving practical objectives in the pursuit of social justice.

ABOUT THE AUTHOR

Michael C. Ennis-McMillan is an associate professor of anthropology in the department of sociology, anthropology, and social work at Skidmore College in Saratoga Springs, New York. He earned his bachelor's of science in biology in 1985 from Northern Michigan University in Marquette, and his master's degree in anthropology in 1994 and his doctorate in anthropology in 1998 from Michigan State University in East Lansing. Intensive fieldwork for this case study took place between 1993 and 1996, with shorter summer fieldwork conducted between 2000 and 2003. From September 2001 through June 2002, Dr. Ennis-McMillan was a researcher-in-residence at the Center for U.S.–Mexican Studies at the University of California in San Diego. The fellowship supported a major writing project as well as his preliminary work on *A Precious Liquid*.

Dr. Ennis-McMillan continues his research in Mexico and more recently has been conducting ethnographic research on political and cultural aspects of drinking water issues in upstate New York. He teaches courses in cultural anthropology, medical anthropology, environmental anthropology, Mexican cultures, and Latin America. He also participates in Skidmore's interdisciplinary programs in environmental studies, international affairs, and Latin American studies.

ABOUT THIS CASE STUDY

This case study examines the question of what it means for rural Mexicans and for us to "suffer from water." The people of La Purificación, a village in the Valley of Mexico, place a special value on a clean and safe water supply. In managing a piped water system, this community has successfully resisted external forces that might jeopardize good maintenance and equitable distribution of their water. Their success is closely linked to tradition, specifically a religious and civil *cargo* system that serves as a leveling mechanism to ensure access to water for every household. In capitalist water systems, access to water is based on ability to pay, thus promoting commodification and overconsumption. In La Purificación participation and service to the community determine eligibility for water, thus promoting conservation and responsible use of the water supply. On a global scale this case illustrates that problems of water scarcity and water quality do not lend themselves to free-market solutions and that strategies to promote conservation and development should be framed in the context of culturally mediated efficiencies.

John A. Young
Series Editor
Emeritus Professor of Anthropology
Oregon State University
Jyoung@oregonstate.edu

Preface

My primary purpose for writing *A Precious Liquid* is to convey the importance of cultural dimensions of drinking water issues. After I completed my initial research in Mexico in 1993, I examined other anthropological studies about drinking water. Although some fine work has been completed on this topic, I discovered that little research has focused specifically on the anthropology of drinking water management. On the one hand, I was excited to begin developing a research topic about which I could make a unique contribution. On the other hand, I became troubled that the few studies that anthropologists had completed had not been incorporated into the international development literature. Furthermore, reports on water-related health issues tend to appear in specialty journals rather than in publications for a more general audience. I was especially troubled to return to the United States and continue hearing stereotypes and misconceptions about Mexicans and their water practices. What kind of contribution could I make to anthropological scholarship and, at the same time, engage readers in a broader public discussion?

That is where Barbara Rose Johnston and John Young came into the picture. Barbara is an anthropologist who has worked extensively on applied anthropology issues related to water and environmental justice. She suggested that I consider publishing my work as a case study in this new series edited by John Young. I talked with John and found out that he wanted to develop a new anthropology book series about contemporary social issues. I thought a case study on water would fit perfectly with John's vision.

In *A Precious Liquid,* readers encounter the typical features of an anthropological study of a Mexican community. Readers explore familiar topics, such as fiestas, *cargo* systems, family patterns, and traditional forms of resource management. At the same time, the case allows readers to explore drinking water issues that have not received much attention in the form of an ethnography to date. The case study presents the information in a personal way so that the readers can better understand why some Mexicans feel so strongly about drinking water as a part of their historical and cultural heritage and why they engage in collective efforts to protect a life-sustaining resource. I hope that this personal approach will provoke readers to consider the implications of a world where environmental and social factors increasingly threaten water resources.

Teaching anthropology has also motivated me to write a book that would be accessible to college students, particularly those with interests in anthropology, international health, environmental studies, and Latin America. The case study also provides interesting material for students focusing on gender, religion, or family dynamics. When I present my research in class, my students become intrigued by the possibility of using an anthropological perspective to think about water issues and other important contemporary problems. Chapter 2 outlines why water has become a pressing international issue and demonstrates why an anthropological perspective is important to consider if we hope to reduce human suffering and environmental degradation. Thus, instructors may want to use this case study as part of an introductory course in anthropology or as part of a more advanced interdisciplinary course, such as environmental studies and Latin American studies, in which students have little prior background in anthropology. More advanced anthropology courses will want to supplement the text with work that more extensively discusses theories in medical anthropology, ecological anthropology, or Latin American anthropology.

In addition to theoretical perspectives in anthropology, *A Precious Liquid* includes information about fieldwork methods. Readers will see that I have purposely included myself in the text and photographs to give students concrete examples of how an anthropologist collects information while living among a group of people in a foreign setting. Thus students will learn about basic research methods, such as building rapport, using participant observation, and interviewing. This focus on research methods should prove useful to students who will have to deal with water issues in whatever country they find themselves, whether during study abroad or personal travels. This case study invites students to apply an anthropological perspective to water issues in any setting. Over the years, I have had a number of students focus on water for independent study projects while studying abroad in places like Bolivia, Madagascar, and India. The book has a comparative perspective that allows students to develop questions about issues other groups face related to water quality, quantity, and distribution.

The case study includes many photographs of the setting and of the residents engaged in water management. This visual anthropology perspective gives readers a better understanding of the collective actions residents take to manage the water system, install and maintain pipes and tanks, confront debtors, and deal with the hardships associated with water shortages. I invite readers to examine closely the photographs and reflect on what seems to be happening in each photograph. This can help readers challenge preconceived ideas and misconceptions based on limited access to visual images of daily life in Mexico.

This case study also includes a brief glossary of Spanish words used most often in the text. Some of the terms are specific to Mexico and to water management and are not part of the vocabulary students typically learn in foreign language courses. I prefer to use the Spanish terms in the text so that readers learn the vocabulary in context. This approach reinforces the connection between language and culture and shows the importance of learning cultural perspectives on environmental issues. Although the word *agua* easily translates as water in English, other terms do not translate so easily. The glossary will allow readers to follow and learn important local terms.

ACKNOWLEDGMENTS

Writing this book has been an extremely rewarding and challenging project. The support and guidance of family, friends, colleagues, and institutions in Mexico and the United States proved invaluable. When I flip through the pages of this book, I recall many faces and voices and feel fortunate to have had so many people take an interest in my exploration of the cultural aspects of drinking water in Mexico.

I am deeply grateful to the residents of La Purificación Tepetitla for their ongoing support. I know it can be challenging to invite a foreign anthropologist into a community, but los Purifiqueños always supplied good cheer and wise counsel as I visited their homes, asked endless questions, and took hundreds of photographs. I feel fortunate that they always invite me back. I am especially grateful to Amelia Villalobos Esparza and Sara Esparza Uribe for allowing me to be a part of their family during my fieldwork. I also give a special thanks to my friend Adolfo González Velázquez who helped me begin my studies in the community. I also thank several friends who spent considerable time explaining many of the issues I analyze in this book: Manuel de la Cruz Díaz, Manuel Miranda Velázquez, Ana María Sanchez Rosas, Sara Velázquez Sánchez, and Trini Velázquez Sánchez. The list of names of everyone who supported my research is too long to mention here, but know that I will follow the advice of one good friend who asked that I always carry fond memories of my time with los Purifiqueños—not only in my notebooks, computer files, and photo albums, but also in my heart. Rest assured, friends, that I do.

I have many other people to thank on both sides of the U.S.–Mexico border. First, I give a big thank you to Barbara Rose Johnston for recommending my work for this book series, and I give a very big thank you to John Young for his careful editing and patience. I had a few rough periods that made it difficult to finish some of the writing, and Barbara and John together gently and kindly nudged me along. Thanks also to Lin Marshall and all those at Thomson Wadsworth for their assistance and goodwill.

In Mexico, I have had wonderful support from the faculty and students affiliated with the Programa Posgraduado en Antropología Social, Departamento de Ciencias Sociales y Políticas, Universidad Iberoamericana in Mexico City. I particularly thank Profesora Carmen Viqueira Landa for supervising my first fieldwork in northern Acolhuacan and for guiding my ongoing analysis of water issues. Thanks also to Carmen Bueno, Roger Magazine, Roberto Melville, Jacinta Palerm, and David Robichaux. In the United States, an earlier phase of the research and writing benefited from colleagues and friends in the department of anthropology at Michigan State University, particularly Eufracio C. Abaya, David Dwyer, Janice Harper, Laurie Medina, Ann V. Millard, Harry Raulet, and Scott Whiteford. This book has also benefited from the wise counsel of other scholars interested in health and water in Latin America, particularly Vivienne Bennett, Lynn Morgan, and Linda Whiteford.

More recently, Skidmore College has provided a nurturing environment that allowed me to bring this project to completion. All my colleagues in the department of sociology, anthropology, and social work have been supportive of my work, and I particularly thank Jill Sweet and Susan Walzer for their friendship and encouragement during those hard moments of writing. Many Skidmore students also contributed to the work with their comments and suggestions. For research and editorial assistance, I particularly thank Darcy Brennan, Tim Karis, and Chlöe Waters. Special thanks to Leah Goldberg and Erin DeCou for joining me in a semester-long reading group where we worked in a truly collaborative manner. Leah and Erin read the entire draft of the manuscript and offered useful suggestions that improved the final version.

This long-term ethnographic project was made possible with generosity of several institutions. The initial dissertation fieldwork was supported by the following: an International Predissertation Fellowship from the Social Science Research Council and the American Council of Learned Societies with funds provided by the Ford Foundation; Foreign Area Studies Language Fellowships from the Center for Latin American and Caribbean Studies and the Center for Advanced Studies in International Development, Michigan State University, with funds provided by the United States Department of Education, Title VI Program; a Dissertation Fellowship from the Inter-American Foundation; a Small Grant for Dissertation Research from the Wenner-Gren Foundation for Anthropological Research; and dissertation writing funds from the College of Social Science and the Dean of the Graduate School, Michigan State University. I am grateful to Skidmore College for awarding several faculty development grants to conduct follow-up research in the summers and for granting me a sabbatical, which gave me the time needed to research and begin writing this book. I am also grateful to the Center for U.S.–Mexican Studies, University of California in San Diego, which provided funds and space that allowed me to begin the hard work of putting the book together. It is heartening to know that these institutions see scholarly and practical merit in the anthropological study of water issues in Mexico.

Chapter 6 is revised from "La Vida del Pueblo: Women and Household Water Management in the Valley of Mexico," which appeared as a chapter in *Opposing Currents: The Politics of Water and Gender in Latin America*, edited by Vivienne Bennett, Sonia Dávila-Poblete, and María Nieves Rico (2005, 137–153). Chapter 7 is revised from "Suffering from Water: Social Origins of Bodily Distress in a Mexican Community," which appeared in *Medical Anthropology Quarterly* (2001a, 368–390). I am grateful for permission to reproduce revised works as part of this case study.

Last but not least, I thank family and friends for their love and support over the course of this long project. For support through the earlier phases of research and writing, I especially thank Bunny Ennis, Kelly Ennis, Pam Harnack, Jay Kleiman, and Jerod Scholten. Special thanks to Saul Bachiller for the support, encouragement, and companionship that helped me make the final push.

As with any book, the author makes the final decisions. The limitations, errors, and views presented in this case study are my own and not those of the individuals and institutions listed above.

Thank you all. Gracias a todos.

A Precious Liquid

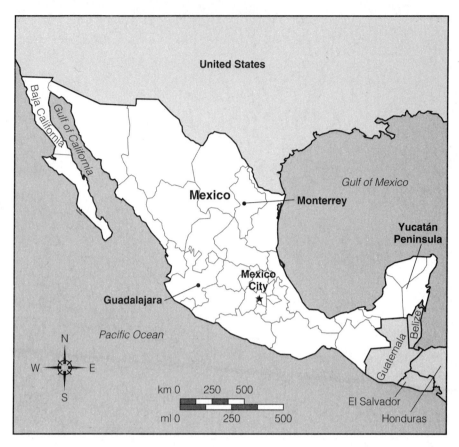

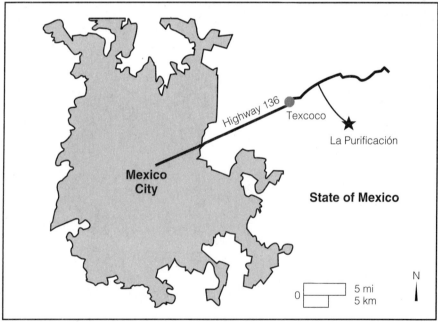

Figure 0.1 Map of Mexico indicating the location of La Purificación. The upper map shows the location of Mexico City in the central highlands of Mexico. The lower map shows the boundaries of Mexico City. La Purificación is located about 20 miles to the west of the center of Mexico City in the State of Mexico.

1/Introduction
A Precious Liquid

WELCOME TO THE PARADISE OF LA PURIFICACIÓN

Nearly 6,000 residents live in La Purificación, a community in the northeastern foothills of the Valley of Mexico about 20 miles from the center of Mexico City (see Figure 0.1). A large metal arch over the community's main road greets passersby with the message "Welcome to the Paradise of La Purificación" (see Figure 1.1). Some vehicles have bumper stickers that read "I (love) the Paradise of La Purificación," with the word *love* represented by a red heart. Indeed, while not claiming to live in an ideal setting, residents regularly tell visitors that the community has a better quality of life than nearby Mexico City and other urban areas of the heavily populated Valley of Mexico. Traveling farther down La Purificación's main road, however, a visitor might encounter other messages that are not so welcoming, such as a sign posted in the main plaza that reads: "NOTICE. Don't be fooled with the sale of properties that don't have drinking water or sewage service. More information in the municipal offices of La Purificación." Rather than referring to a paradise, this sort of sign reflects mounting concerns about how to manage the local supply of drinking water, a scarce and precious liquid in Mexico.

One cannot visit La Purificación long without appreciating the enormous emphasis that people place on water for drinking and other basic necessities. In this semiarid and mountainous environment, water for household use is a scarce and costly resource, one that people talk about daily. Usually, at some point in a discussion about local water issues, someone will remind listeners that "Water is a precious liquid!" or "Water is a vital liquid!" and that "Water is life!" Residents talk about water as people talk about the earth's other precious resources, such as diamonds, gold, and oil. This view of water contrasts with views of water in the United States and other industrialized countries, where water, until recently, has been taken for granted as an abundant and easily renewable resource. In La Purificación, however, people have a long history of living with water scarcity and relying on a culturally specific form of drinking water management. This

Figure 1.1 An arch over the main road leading into the community greets visitors with the message "Welcome to the Paradise of La Purificación."

book examines the cultural aspects of La Purificación's particular drinking water system and explores lessons that we might draw when thinking about critical water issues in other areas of the world.

This anthropological study is based on ethnographic research, which consists of participant observation as well as interviews. Based on over 10 years of research, this ethnographic case study relies on information collected while living in the community for over a year and a half as well as brief visits over several summers. Although an ethnography typically examines a group's whole way of life, my ethnography focuses on specific cultural issues related to how a particular Mexican community manages its drinking water supplies. Along the way, of course, I provide information about many aspects of traditional culture and daily life in La Purificación. Indeed, one of the most rewarding, if not challenging, aspects of my work as an anthropologist has been to relate drinking water issues to other aspects of Mexican culture, such as religion, politics, gender, and economics. By the end of the book, readers will better appreciate the value of using an anthropological approach to understand how culture, in any part of the world, influences the way people use one of earth's most precious resources: water.

CHOOSING A RESEARCH SITE

For any anthropologist, selecting a research site and a topic can be a complex process. In my own case, I did not originally go to Mexico to study drinking water issues. As happens in many anthropological projects, my research agenda

Figure 1.2 La Purificación sits within a small valley surrounded by hills.

was shaped by a combination of chance, opportunity, and interest. People in La Purificación often asked why I chose to study their community. Half joking, I usually explained that I did not choose to study drinking water issues in La Purificación. Rather, the topic chose me.

Before starting my anthropology research in central Mexico, I had only been to Mexico once for a two-week backpacking trip to the Yucatán Peninsula, which lies deep in the country's southeastern region. Later, after beginning a graduate program in anthropology, I decided to do research on a medical anthropology topic in Mexico. My advisors thought it would be good for me to have some ethnographic research training from Mexican anthropologists before undertaking a major research project in the country. In 1993, as a graduate student, I attended a summer anthropology field school run by Mexican anthropologists from the Universidad Iberoamericana in Mexico City. The field school is located in Tepetalaoztoc and has been used since the 1960s to train anthropologists to carry out ethnographic research (Viqueira 1990, 1992; Wolf 1981). I was pleased to be accepted to the field school because the training would allow me to improve my Spanish language skills and learn how to do ethnographic research in Mexico. Actual training in the field while living in a community also promised to give me the time to develop more suitable ideas for a longer dissertation research project.

In addition to receiving invaluable training, I went to Mexico to test out several research ideas. I was interested in developing a project that would combine my interests in medical anthropology and environmental anthropology. Medical anthropologists typically study traditional healers and medicines, but I wanted to explore other topics and make a new contribution to anthropological knowledge.

Medical anthropologists had been discussing the need for more research on how political and economic forces influence access to and control of clean water and other natural resources that influence human health (Baer et al. 2003; Harper 2002; Morgan 1993; Whiteford 1997). It seemed interesting and important to develop a project that would advance cross-cultural knowledge related to environmental health issues. In 1993, water issues were at the top of my list of topics to consider, but I was also interested in environmental health issues related to deforestation, urbanization, food security, and air pollution.

As part of the summer field school, students were required to live with a family and conduct a brief project in a community near the field school. I teamed up with Pablo, a Mexican graduate student, and explored several communities. One day in June, Pablo and I visited La Purificación. When we arrived at the Catholic church in the community's central plaza, we discovered that a mass was being held in the middle of the day. A yellow tarp hung over the entrance to the church and the façade was decorated with flowers and banners. A group of musicians with clarinets, coronets, drums, and a tuba played a tune outside the church. We had stumbled upon a Mexican fiesta! It turned out we had arrived during Corpus Christi, La Purificación's second largest annual fiesta.

Just as we were curious about the elaborate fiesta, people too were curious about our presence. My intermediate Spanish skills did not allow me to make out people's comments, but I noticed a group of men outside the church looking our way and laughing. Later Pablo told me that somebody said, "Look. The devils have arrived." As outsiders, we were easy targets for this kind of joke.

Months later, I looked back on how out of place we must have seemed to local residents. The church was full of residents who knew each other. Pablo and

Figure 1.3 Musicians play near the Catholic church during an annual fiesta.

I—each fair-skinned guys with glasses and beards—easily stood out amid a crowd of brown faces. In addition, we were dressed in a manner that was out of ordinary for the community. On that hot summer day, we each wore large straw hats, dusty jeans, and hiking boots. We each dangled a camera from our necks, carried backpacks with bottled water and snacks, and wrote in our notebooks. Although not quite devils, we certainly must have presented an unfamiliar sight to locals. Why would anybody assume we were anthropology graduate students and not tourists, Protestant missionaries, government officials, news reporters, or agricultural researchers? It was the first of many encounters that reminded me that I was a stranger and outsider. The incident at the church was also a useful lesson for any anthropologist hoping to work in a tight-knit community. I had to expect that, no matter the community, it would take some time to learn to fit in and have people become accustomed to my presence.

Intrigued by the fiesta, I returned the following day. Fiestas have long been the subject of anthropological research, particularly among indigenous groups in rural areas of Mexico's southern states of Oaxaca and Chiapas. Fiestas involve a mixture of Catholic ritual with local customs and are central aspects of community life in Mexico and other Latin American countries (Stephen and Dow 1990). La Purificación had originally been an indigenous community and most residents recognize some sort of indigenous heritage. Nevertheless, today, La Purificación is not considered an indigenous community. Since the early 1900s, the community had become more oriented toward national Mexican culture. Residents do not speak Nahuatl or other indigenous languages and instead live their lives as Spanish-speaking Catholics who identify themselves as *campesinos* or rural people who rely on agriculture for part of their livelihood.

I had not expected to see such an elaborate fiesta system in a nonindigenous community located in an urbanizing area several miles outside of Mexico City. The group of religious officers who organizes the annual fiestas is called a *mayordomía;* each male religious officer is called a *mayordomo* and each female officer is called a *mayordoma*. Because La Purificación's *mayordomías* seemed more active than I would have expected based on other anthropology research, I thought that a brief ethnographic study of a particular fiesta would make an ideal summer project. I found out that La Purificación celebrates a smaller fiesta in July, so I decided to study the customs associated with preparing and celebrating that fiesta. I never intended to continue studying fiestas after that summer field school, but what I imagined to be the real anthropology research project would have to wait until after I had gained the necessary language and research skills. Up to that point, it never occurred to me that water would eventually become the focus of a more extensive research project.

DISCOVERING AN ANTHROPOLOGICAL PUZZLE

The following week, Pablo and I both found housing with different families. I stayed with Amelia, who was in her 60s at the time, and her mother, Sarita, who was in her 90s. After finding lodging, Pablo and I introduced ourselves to local authorities and explained our plans to study the history and customs of the community. The initial phase of the ethnographic study involved building rapport.

I walked around the community, took pictures of buildings and scenery, and greeted people. Eventually, word spread that I meant no harm and that I was interested in staying longer than a few days. Residents became more open to talking to me and wanted to find out more about me, a curious-looking newcomer. Within a week, I settled in and began organizing my brief summer project.

To learn more about the local fiestas, I began hanging out at the church. Adolfo was one of the first people I met at the church. I saw him watering plants in the garden one day and struck up a conversation about the church and the previous fiesta. It turned out that Adolfo was not only a mayordomo but also a *fiscal,* the title given to the head fiesta organizers. He was in his early 30s and had short, dark hair and a mustache. That summer, he usually wore dark blue or black clothing because he and his family were in mourning for his maternal grandmother who had passed away a few months earlier. Adolfo seemed pleased that I wanted to know more about the fiestas, a tradition that had been particularly meaningful to his grandmother.

Adolfo and I worked together throughout the summer. He allowed me to ask questions, write notes, take pictures, and learn a great deal about local traditions and customs. As a head of a mayordomía, he helped organize a group of men and women who were elected that year to hold a religious office. Each year, the community elects 40 people to these religious offices. Adolfo headed one group of 20 people in a mayordomía, and another person headed the other group of 20 people in a separate mayordomía. Multiple fiestas are celebrated over the year and include two large fiestas—one for the patron virgin in February and the

Figure 1.4 Adolfo the fiscal. *Adolfo (third from the right) stands with his mother, brothers, and sister near an image of the Virgin of the Candelaria, during the annual fiesta for the patron of La Purificación.*

other for Corpus Christi celebrations in the summer—and a number of smaller celebrations, including Holy Week and Easter in the spring, Day of the Dead ceremonies in November, and celebrations for the patron saints of two small chapels in October and December. The two larger fiestas take months of preparation and the entire community is invited to participate in the Catholic masses, processions, meals, dances, fireworks, and other celebratory activities that take place over several days at a time. Consequently, the celebrations are elaborate affairs and require a great deal of organization and resources to carry out each year. The group of men and women regularly cleaned and maintained the church, decorated the church for festivals, collected annual fees from community members, and, most importantly, organized the fiesta activities.

One day, I talked to Adolfo in more depth about how people were elected to be mayordomos and mayordomas. I told him I was impressed that so many people voluntarily gave their time, money, and labor to take care of the church and organize the annual fiestas for a year. Adolfo explained that all heads of the family must take on this religious office when it is their turn.

"So, everybody has to be a mayordomo or mayordoma when it is their turn?" I asked Adolfo.

"Yes, that's right," he said.

I asked, "And what if somebody doesn't want to do it?"

"Everyone has to accept the position," he responded. "It's the custom."

"Yes, but if somebody refused to be a mayordomo, what would happen?"

"It would look bad," said Adolfo. "We would not let them use the church for weddings or funerals."

"You would not let them use the church? Is that all that would happen?"

"Well," Adolfo added, "We would also cut off their water."

"You cut off their water?" I asked, somewhat surprised.

"Yes, their drinking water. We cut it off if they do not agree to be part of a mayordomía."

Voilà! Adolfo's comment linked religious traditions with water customs. With that piece of ethnographic information, a short summer project about one small fiesta turned into a larger, multiyear study about community-based water management. I began by asking Adolfo and others why they thought it made sense to cut off drinking water from those who refused to sponsor a Catholic festival. The question turned out to be so multifaceted and interesting that the summer project led to more extensive research and has since occupied many of my professional research activities. From an outsider's perspective, the peculiarity of the practice made it seem like a fine anthropological puzzle. When describing the goal of ethnographic work, anthropologists are fond of drawing from T.S. Eliot's idea that all good poetry should make the "strange familiar and the familiar strange." Similarly, all good ethnographic studies should make sense of strange customs and, in turn, make us see how our familiar cultural practices might be viewed as rather peculiar.

In this case, the practice of cutting off drinking water of people who do not sponsor fiestas seemed both unfamiliar and peculiar to me. The custom had not been reported in the anthropological literature about Mexico and it seemed interesting that the fiesta traditions often associated with Mexico's out-of-the-way rural places in the south took place near one of the world's largest cities. An adequate explanation of how and why this occurred required an examination of the local history of water practices and the community's fiesta system. It also raised many questions about how the community currently manages its drinking water system: Who made decisions about who received access to drinking water? Were these decisions fair or was cutting off water an abuse of power by higher-status individuals? How was water related to local religious practices? How did the community maintain this local drinking water system since the 1970s when research has shown that many community-based water systems in developing countries fail within a few years? Did this type of water management lead to unintended social and environmental consequences? These research questions emerged from the setting, which is why I say that the research topic chose me. Nevertheless, as a graduate student seeking to carry out dissertation fieldwork on this topic, I had to justify a more extensive project to my advisors and other anthropologists to obtain permission and funds to carry out the research.

I knew I was onto a good puzzle when some anthropologists responded to my ideas with skepticism. They said that Mexican law does not allow authorities to cut off a household's drinking water supply in this manner. Others questioned whether women were really elected as mayordomas because previous anthropology research, mostly carried out in highland Indian communities of southern Mexico and Guatemala, had reported that only men occupied such religious posts (Chance 1990; Chance and Taylor 1985; DeWalt 1975; Stephen and Dow 1990). Some people even questioned whether I needed to improve my Spanish language skills to understand what was really going on. Most colleagues, however, responded in an encouraging manner, especially Mexican anthropologists who explained that the drinking water customs seem related to the region's rich history of irrigation management. It also seemed that unraveling this puzzle might shed light on the conditions that favor community participation in drinking water projects, a factor that other researchers said was necessary for making such development projects viable in the long run (Cox and Annis 1988; Elmendorf 1981). My professors approved a longer study and several foundations provided research funds to study traditional management of drinking water supplies in Mexico.

I returned to La Purificación in January 1995 and lived there until June 1996. This ethnographic account is largely a result of that fieldwork as well as follow-up research completed during the summers of 2000, 2002, and 2003. Throughout the book, I describe my experiences living and working as an anthropologist in La Purificación. I lived with a family, spoke Spanish most of the time, attended numerous fiestas, and fell in love with homemade tortillas, *mole* sauce, *tlacoyos,* tamales, and other tasty Mexican treats. I interviewed water officials, had numerous conversations about water with local residents, and observed many aspects of drinking water management. I participated in the culture by joining residents as they dug trenches to lay water pipes, hauled rocks to build water tanks, held community meetings about water policies, and discussed their concerns about water in daily conversations. Most of all, I learned to appreciate the cultural complexity of managing scarce water supplies in Mexico.

GLOBAL WATER SCARCITY

La Purificación's water issues are fascinating in their own right, but beyond this community, water is becoming a pressing environmental and health issue in Mexico as well as globally. Thus, my case study is more than an intriguing local story. This ethnographic account speaks to larger issues in a world where water is becoming increasingly scarce for many of the world's population. Moreover, the search for adequate water is, in large measure, a search for equity because growing social inequalities explain why many people suffer from water scarcity, a point that needs to be emphasized more strongly in current discussions about global water issues.

For most of human history, the earth's natural water cycle has provided sufficient fresh water to meet basic human needs. Recent reports from the United Nations and other international organizations, however, have been raising awareness that the world's freshwater supplies are not as abundant or renewable as commonly assumed (see United Nations/World Water Assessment Programme [UN/WWAP] 2003; World Health Organization [WHO] 2000; World Water Commission and World Water Council 2000). These reports note that only about 2.5 percent of the earth's water is not salty, and most of that water is locked in snowcaps and glaciers or in inaccessible places underground. Another part of that fresh water arrives as monsoons, hurricanes, and floods when the water cannot be captured and stored for later use. Consequently, less than 0.1 percent of the earth's water is available for human use and 70 percent of that water is used for irrigation to produce food. As a result, little fresh water remains for daily human consumption. From this perspective, drinking water is indeed a precious liquid.

Clean, safe water is vital for daily human survival as well as for food production and the survival of other species. But fresh water has become severely threatened by a complex set of interrelated factors: population increases, urban growth, industrialization, overconsumption, pollution, inefficient and abusive water practices, unequal distribution, habitat destruction, and global climate change. Across the globe, governments, scientific research institutions, health and development organizations, environmental groups, and other concerned groups have reached a consensus that we are witnessing a worldwide freshwater crisis (Barlow and Clark 2002; DeVilliers 2001; Gleick 1993, 2004; Postel 1992; UN/WWAP 2003; WHO 2000; World Water Commission and World Water Council 2000).

In every country, residential consumption increasingly competes with industry and agriculture for limited, clean water supplies. Although the problem is more severe in developing countries, a majority of the cities in Europe, Canada, and the United States are exploiting groundwater at unsustainable rates. In Central Asia, the Aral Sea, once the world's fourth biggest inland sea, has dried up and become a deadly environmental hazard. The United Nations predicts that water shortages and population increases will likely increase conflicts in arid regions of Africa, Asia, and the Middle East where many rivers, lakes, and aquifers are often shared by more than one country. Across Africa, women spend hours each day hauling a few buckets of water to their households. The Yellow

Figure 1.5 A woman uses a bucket to draw water from a jagüey. *This type of open-air water reservoir was the primary way that residents stored water for household use before installing the piped water system.*

River in China and the Ganges River in India are severely polluted, and major aquifers in both countries are being depleted (Kirby 2004; UN/WWAP 2003). These dramatic examples hint at the growing severity of water scarcity and the threat to human health and well-being.

FOCUS OF THE BOOK

To better understand the human dimensions of water scarcity, this ethnographic study examines how La Purificación manages scarce drinking water supplies in the Valley of Mexico's semiarid and densely populated environment. The next chapter examines in more depth the alarming global trend of people struggling with water scarcity and situates the case study in Mexico's water crisis. Subsequent chapters examine how La Purificación's long-standing struggles over community control of irrigation water have shifted to new struggles that focus on providing a growing community with adequate domestic water supplies. The study focuses on the activities and perspectives of local civil and religious authorities and examines how they make decisions about the community's water supplies. The installation of a piped water system in the 1980s provided people a vital resource and moderated the suffering associated with water scarcity. On the other hand, a better domestic water supply created a new set of social consequences involving conflict and cooperation. I show how residents in La Purificación draw on local traditions and customs to address their concerns about water scarcity and the need for an equitable water distribution system. Overall, residents see drinking water as a collectively shared resource that community members ought to manage and distribute in an equitable fashion to residents who abide by local customary rights and obligations.

As we reflect on the causes and consequences of global water scarcity, this case study highlights the cultural issues involved in the ongoing process of designing, constructing, managing, and maintaining any system for providing adequate potable water for daily needs. A major premise of this book asserts that water scarcity is not simply a natural problem, but is also a social and cultural challenge. The decisions individuals and communities make and the values they place on water affect the way that water cycles through the earth's ecological systems. Solutions will not be solved simply with new technology or new medicines, but necessitate a substantial reorganization of our social and cultural worlds.

In my view, culture consists of sets of meanings and practices people create and use in relation to particular social and material processes. This perspective of culture guides many of the questions explored in subsequent chapters: What does drinking water mean to people? What water management practices make sense to a particular group? How do local politics influence whether water is distributed in an equitable manner? How does a drinking water system relate to particular environmental and social conditions? As I explore these questions, I show how potable water development is shaped by interactions among individuals who sometimes have competing interests related to managing water quality, quantity, and distribution. Community residents make decisions about what new practices to adopt, such as engineering principles and public health standards, and what practices to oppose, such as management techniques that treat water as an unlimited natural resource or as a commodity that ought to be bought and sold in the marketplace. La Purificación's case not only helps us understand the seriousness of water issues but it also points to alternative approaches to managing our world's precious water resources.

2/On the Edge
of a Water Crisis

Residents of La Purificación routinely comment that they enjoy living in their foothill community. Los Purifiqueños, as residents refer to themselves, proudly state that they live in a quiet, tranquil, and relatively crime-free setting where people know each other and live together like one large extended family. Residents take pleasure in saying that, compared to urban areas at lower elevations in the Valley of Mexico, their foothill location is less crowded and has cooler and fresher air, lovely foliage, and charming customs. Los Purifiqueños appreciate the clean air of the foothills, especially when they look below to the valley floor and see Mexico City's smog and haze a few miles off in the distance. It is only on an occasional rare day that the wind clears the air and makes it possible to see across the expanding megalopolis to the distant snowcapped mountains on the other side of the Valley of Mexico. At night, Mexico City's lights brighten the sky for miles around and remind los Purifiqueños that they live on the edge of one of the world's most populated cities. Los Purifiqueños are fond of making puns on their community's name by telling visitors from the city, including anthropologists, that they will become "purified" after breathing the community's "pure air." Everyone smiles at the familiar joke.

Los Purifiqueños also make puns about the community's "purified water," that is local drinking water supplies. This familiar pun also produces knowing grins. Despite such jokes, the community takes a serious stance toward maintaining its access to a relatively clean groundwater supply, even if the water becomes contaminated with coliform bacteria and other microorganisms as it courses through the pipes on the way to individual households. As we will see, residents in La Purificación use the term potable water (*agua potable* in Spanish) to refer to water used for a wide range of daily activities regardless of whether they think the water is suitable for drinking or whether the bacteria counts exceed acceptable limits for drinking water set by public health officials. In this book, I use the terms *drinking water, potable water,* and *domestic water* interchangeably when referring to water that is primarily for household use. Because fresh water is a scarce and highly valued natural resource, los Purifiqueños

Figure 2.1 Dancing during a family gathering.

struggle to maintain control of their local piped water system. Part of their struggles has involved dealing with the threats posed by living on the edge of the
Valley of Mexico and its emerging water shortage.

Although this book focuses on one Mexican community, La Purificación's
water struggles are quite common among communities in rural and peri-urban
areas of Mexico and, indeed, other Latin American countries. This chapter
places La Purificacion's case into a broader context by examining the growing
threats to the world's freshwater supplies. We all are living on the edge of a
water crisis that, along with global climate change, is one of the world's most
immediate and pressing environmental problems. Drawing on research in medical anthropology and environmental anthropology, this chapter ends with a discussion of anthropological perspectives that can help us better understand the
cultural dimensions of community-based drinking water management.

THE WORLD'S WATER CRISIS

It may seem astonishing that the human population is dealing with an emerging
water crisis, because water covers nearly two-thirds of the earth's surface. After
all, we live on a blue planet. Most of the earth's water, however, is too salty for
human consumption or irrigation. The small amount of fresh water that exists on
earth flows through the physical environment in a regular cycle. This hydrologic
cycle starts when water molecules from the ocean evaporate into the air and
become separated from the surrounding salts and other impurities in the ocean.
When moist air becomes cooler, water molecules condense and fall to earth as

rain or snow. Arid and semiarid areas, which cover about one-third of the earth's landmass, receive little rainfall or snowfall. On land, water collects on the surface to form snowcaps, glaciers, lakes, rivers, ponds, and other wetlands. Water also percolates into the earth and forms aquifers, which are underground pools of water trapped among layers of clay, rock, and sand. Groundwater is extracted by digging or drilling wells and pumping water to the surface. The natural hydrologic cycle allows aquifers to be recharged when water fills an aquifer at the same rate as it is extracted. Water becomes purified as it filters through the hydrologic cycle. A large volume of water—either as surface water or groundwater pumped to the surface—eventually drains back to the ocean and completes the cycle.

For most of human history until about 1700, less than one billion people lived on the planet. That number increased to two billion people by 1900 and exceeded six billion people by 2000. With a fixed volume of fresh water on the planet, this population increase puts pressure on water systems and has created what the United Nations and other international organizations term the world's water crisis. The international community has reached a consensus on the need to recognize the water crisis and adopt new approaches to managing freshwater resources (Gleick 2004; UN 1992; UN/WWAP 2003; World Health Organization and United Nations Children's Fund [WHO/UNICEF] 2000; World Water Commission and World Water Council 2000). Reports estimate that more than 1.2 billion people—one-fifth of the world's population—currently suffer from unhealthy and inadequate supplies of water for drinking and other basic necessities. Nearly half the world's population lacks safe sanitation. By 2025, nearly 9 billion people will be living on the planet and 2.3 billion people—more than one-quarter of the total population—will have inadequate access to water to meet basic needs. Furthermore, over half of the people in developing countries will lack access to adequate potable water. In other words, we are witnessing an increase in both the number and proportion of people living with inadequate water quality and quantity. Thirst, like hunger, afflicts billions of people.

In numerous places throughout the world, poor-quality water supplies compromise health and generate suffering (Gleick 2004). Water-related diseases account for a significant amount of morbidity and mortality, especially among infants and children in developing countries (WHO/UNICEF 2000). Some estimates suggest that one-half of people in developing countries suffer from water-related health problems due to toxins, as well as viruses, bacteria, and parasitic infections. Leading water-related health problems include diarrhea, schistosomiasis, dengue fever, intestinal worm infections, malaria, onchocerciasis (river blindness), and trachoma. Development programs have educated people about washing hands and purifying drinking water, installed piped water and sanitation systems to isolate human and animal waste from drinking water sources, and provided pharmaceuticals to prevent and cure water-related illnesses. In addition to biological pathogens, many populations suffer from increased exposure to water polluted with salts, heavy metals, volatile organic compounds, radioactive compounds, and other hazardous materials. Many new chemical pollutants can be extremely hazardous and take years, if not decades, to clean up.

Water quality, however, is only part of the story. For many people, the issues go beyond purifying water and adopting hygienic practices. In many developing countries, people struggle simply to gain access to a basic supply of water for daily needs regardless of whether the water is suitable for drinking. The average person living in a moderate climate needs a minimum of 1.3 gallons of water per day to drink and a minimum of 13 gallons of water per day for drinking, bathing, preparing food, and disposing of human waste (Gleick 1996). A minimum of 50 gallons per day allows an individual to lead a much more healthy and comfortable life. A large number of people live with less than these minimum amounts. The problem is getting worse, especially for people living in dry and densely populated regions where it is difficult to manage water resources (UN/WWAP 2003).

In addition to threats to water quality and quantity, an uneven distribution of water compounds the freshwater crisis. Over half of the world's freshwater supplies are located in a few nations—mostly northern industrialized, developed nations that make up only about one-fifth of the world's population. Anthropologists Barbara Rose Johnston and John Donahue (1998) have noted that higher-income, urban dwellers consume the majority of the world's freshwater supplies and that the inequity within and between nations has generated environmental injustices and increased social conflicts. In the next few decades, limited water, inequitable resource distribution, and increased demands will intensify conflicts between beneficial uses of water and the need to protect the environment. Water is the world's blue gold (Barlow and Clark 2002). Like the conflicts surrounding competition for oil in the twentieth century, we are seeing regional competition over precious water resources lead to larger social conflicts and disorder in the twenty-first century (DeVilliers 1999; Postel 1996; Shiva 2003). Some analysts argue that lack of access to water is emerging as a widespread human rights issue (Gleick 1999).

Population increases and increased standards of living put more pressure on limited water supplies for both household consumption and for food production. Urban growth and industrialization increase the demand for water and generate pollution. Likewise, urban growth destroys open spaces, lakes, rivers, and wetlands, which are necessary for naturally purifying water as well as for creating buffers against floods. Environmental destruction endangers existing freshwater supplies and threatens many animal and plant species that rely on fresh water. Lacking sufficient fresh water, farmers in developing countries increasingly irrigate crops with untreated wastewater, which further increases risk of exposure to waterborne diseases. In rural areas, inefficient irrigation systems waste a tremendous amount of water and release salts, fertilizers, pesticides, herbicides, and other pollutants to the environment.

Many populations depend on groundwater supplies, but an alarming number of aquifers are being degraded. In many areas, water is pumped out of aquifers at a faster rate than can be replenished. If the aquifer is not recharged with water, the water volume decreases and leads to an overdraft situation. Furthermore, urban growth increases the amount of paved and covered surface areas, which decreases the ability of water to percolate underground and recharge aquifers. Overpumping an aquifer can also lead to land subsidence, which is the settling or sinking of the ground. Subsidence can occur when water is removed from underground, thereby reducing support for the earth's surface. If the clay, rocks, and sand that form the aquifer become compressed, the ground settles gradually or, in some cases, sinks suddenly and creates fissures or sinkholes in the earth. Land subsidence reduces the underground space available for storing water, which makes water less available for areas that rely on underground supplies. If less space is available to store water underground, then wastewater, storm water, and runoff from irrigation can no longer percolate into the ground and recharge aquifers. A decreased amount of water underground increases an area's vulnerability to drought. Similarly, if storm water cannot percolate underground, then it stays on the surface and increases the risk and severity of flooding. In some coastal areas, depleted aquifers fill with salt water from the ocean. Saltwater intrusion increases the cost of water treatment and can seriously harm aquifers and surrounding freshwater ecosystems.

In addition to these immediate threats, global climate change will likely exacerbate water problems. Global climate change will increase the portion of the world's population living in warmer settings and thereby increase demand for daily amounts of water. Increased global temperatures will also increase water temperatures, which will accelerate evaporation rates of freshwater supplies and harm freshwater organisms. At the same time, melting snowcaps could increase ocean levels, flooding coastal areas and intensifying saltwater intrusion of aquifers. Altered weather patterns will likely affect rainfall, snowfall, and runoff and may increase the frequency and severity of floods and droughts.

Current threats to fresh water are immediate and becoming more severe. Most of these problems occur in every country of the world and put clean domestic water supplies for billions of people in competition with other beneficial uses of water, including habitat protection, irrigation, hydropower, industrial production, transportation, recreation, and tourism (Gleick 2000). We live in a world where we can no longer take water for granted.

MEXICO'S WATER CRISIS

Mexico reflects many of the world trends in freshwater issues. Like all countries, Mexico has taken steps to improve water and sanitation services. Mexico's 1917 Constitution lists water as a federal guarantee for all citizens. Since that time, national programs have focused considerable attention on improving domestic water systems. In 1992, Mexico passed a new national water law in an effort to improve water services. In some respects, Mexico ranks rather high among developing countries in terms of the population with access to piped water supplies and sanitation services. Mexico has a population of over 102 million people, making it the second most populous country in Latin America, after Brazil (CountryWatch 2005). According to the Pan American Health Organization (PAHO), over 87 percent of Mexico's population have easy access to some form of domestic water service. Easy access refers to the ability of a household to provide 10 to 13 gallons of water per inhabitant per day from a source that delivers water directly to the house or from a source not more than about 1,300 feet (400 meters) from the house (PAHO 2001).

Despite some of these efforts, Mexico's water development programs appear less promising than planned, especially for poorer rural and peri-urban communities. Anthropologists have noted that Mexico's water crisis is an immediate and growing environmental and cultural problem (Melville and Cirelli 2000). Water resources are scarce and polluted in Mexico's arid northern states, and inaccessible and of poor quality in the semiarid and tropical areas of the central and southern states. In urban areas, untreated sewage and industrial waste pollute lakes and rivers. Water quality problems create a significant amount of diseases, including new health problems due to heavy metals and other industrial pollutants. In addition, only about 44 percent of Mexicans live in households with connections to a sewerage system. Although systems for piping water have helped, most Mexicans regularly deal with water shortages, aquifer overexploitation, subsidence, saltwater intrusion, and industrial pollution.

In 2001, Mexico's president declared that water problems pose a significant threat to national security. The 13 percent of Mexicans who report having no easy access to potable water represent over 13 million people. In many areas, programs have tended to restrict the installation of piped water systems in poor communities in favor of increasing water supply to wealthier urban neighborhoods, the industrial sector, and large-scale irrigation projects. As a result, 90 percent of the urban population report having access to piped water, but only 55 percent of the rural population report having adequate access (PAHO 2001; Restrepo 1995). Furthermore, such reports focus on who has piped water, but the reports say little about the deteriorated water quality, increasing water shortages, water rationing, and the rising cost of the water, which are significant issues for many Mexicans.

The Valley of Mexico experiences some of the most dramatic aspects of the water crisis. In fact, the valley's environmental and health problems are related to

Figure 2.2 The center of Mexico City. In this picture, the large open space in the middle is the Zócalo, the city's central plaza. The national palace is the long building facing the Zócalo, and the Catholic cathedral's bell towers appear on the left.

the nation's worst water shortages and water pollution as well as problems associate with air pollution, habitat destruction, and other environmental problems (Kasperson et al. 1996; Restrepo 1995). Mexico City, the nation's capital, and its surrounding metropolitan area dominate the valley. When the Spaniards arrived over 500 years ago, they encountered the Aztec's capital city, Tenochtitlan, surrounded by lakes. Since that time, the lakes have been drained and the surrounding forests have been cleared. As Mexico City grew in size, the water problems also grew. The valley has limited water sources and, since the beginning of the twentieth century, has suffered from inadequate amounts of fresh water. Today, at least 20 million people, or almost 20 percent of the national population, live in the Valley of Mexico, which makes the area one of the densest concentrations of people in the world. Mexico City has overconsumed the valley's groundwater supplies and created an alarming incidence of subsidence.

We can see the effects of subsidence, for example, by visiting Mexico City's central plaza, the Zócalo. When the Spaniards built the massive Catholic cathedral in the Zócalo, a set of stairs led up to the entrance several yards above ground. In the 1500s, the ascent symbolized a journey toward God and the heavens. Today the ground has sunk so low that visitors walk *down* a few steps to enter the cathedral. I am not sure what this descent symbolizes, but it does reflect the deterioration of the city's aquifer. Subsidence has also reduced underground space to hold wastewater and storm water. The excess water has contaminated clean water supplies and increased flooding in the valley.

Population increases, subsidence, and water scarcity have led to the development of one of the world's most elaborate and costly hydraulic infrastructures to carry water into Mexico City from distant sources. The city depends on water

Figure 2.3 The Catholic cathedral in Mexico City's Zócalo, demonstrating the effects of subsidence. Visitors must take steps down to enter the cathedral.

from the valley's mountain springs as well as lakes, rivers, and aquifers located hundreds of miles outside the valley (Melville 1996a, 1996b). Mexico City also instituted programs to export its untreated and partially treated wastewater to rural areas for irrigation in exchange for transporting cleaner water from mountain springs to the city. As I explain later, los Purifiqueños constantly worry that they will be pressured to participate in such programs to satisfy Mexico City's enormous thirst. To date, La Purificación and nearby communities have strongly rejected plans to transport their fresh water to urban areas or to allow urban wastewater to be transported to the foothills.

Some argue that water scarcity in the Valley of Mexico has become an environmental injustice, if not a human rights issue, because the unequal water distribution disproportionately affects poorer and less powerful groups (Restrepo 1995). Mexico City and surrounding areas have many poor areas with households that fall short of having access to 13 gallons of water per person per day, whereas households in wealthier neighborhoods receive over 10 times that amount. Furthermore, municipal governments often subsidize water for wealthier neighborhoods, especially in neighborhoods that receive piped municipal supplies. People living in poorer neighborhoods not only receive less water but they pay up to 25 times more per gallon of water than people in wealthier neighborhoods. People living in poorer areas often rely on water trucks, which can be an extremely costly way to obtain water (see Figure 2.4). Many poorer households cannot afford to fill more than a 50-gallon metal drum with water every few days (Flores 1995; García Lascuráin 1995). Water scarcity especially affects women who expend considerable time, money, and labor ensuring their households have adequate water supplies to meet basic daily needs.

Figure 2.4 A water truck delivers drinking water (agua potable) *to a household.*

A later chapter elaborates how water scarcity affects women's lives in La Purificación. Many women explained that they actively participate in water issues because they depend on water to cook meals and wash clothes for their families. Women literally feel the burden of water scarcity when they have to ration water, carry water long distances, or use scarce household funds to pay for water from an expensive water truck. When the water delivery system breaks down, some women face the unpleasant tradeoff of buying food instead of water. Water, they told me, is more than simply a beverage. It is a vital liquid around which daily life revolves—cooking, cleaning, washing clothes, and bathing. "Water is life," explained Sarita. "With no water, there is no life."

TROUBLED WATERS IN THE UNITED STATES

For comparative purposes, let us turn to Mexico's neighbor to the north. Living in a developed industrial country, most U.S. residents might be inclined to associate drinking water problems with developing countries. Indeed, before leaving for Mexico, how many travelers hear the warning "Don't drink the water"? Over the years, I have grown tired of hearing this statement because the speakers usually assume that Mexico's water problems are due primarily to poor water quality and lack of a modern water infrastructure like the one we supposedly have in the United States. It is true that the United States has large supplies of groundwater and surface water and low rates of water-related diseases. Like many developed countries, our water technology, medical science, and public health programs have helped solve many drinking water and sanitation problems. The United States has spent billions of dollars on a massive water and sanitation infrastructure and has developed advanced water treatment systems. Today, nearly 100 percent of the population can easily access clean drinking water (PAHO 2001). Most U.S. residents can expect to go almost anywhere in the nation and turn on a water tap or use a shower and have plenty of clean drinkable water—even if the water is not always intended for drinking.

Not surprisingly, the United States has one of the highest rates of water consumption in the world. The average person in the United States uses between 50 to 100 gallons per day for drinking, cooking, bathing, and watering the yard (Gleick 2000). Most people expect access to high-quality drinking water as a beverage, but we regularly use much more of that clean, fresh, sparkling, cold water to flush our toilets, wash our cars, water our grass, and clean our sidewalks and patios. We also expect the same sort of water use for our golf courses, hotels, and parkways. Whereas some households in poorer areas of Mexico struggle to provide five gallons of water per person per day, the average U.S. household uses almost 100 gallons per day to flush toilets! The different patterns of water consumption are not simply a matter of ecological differences. Along the U.S.–Mexico border, the average water consumption in U.S. municipalities is 40 percent greater than in Mexican municipalities on the other side (Westerhoff 2000). In the midst of such abundance and purity, it becomes easy for U.S. residents to imagine that Mexico and other developing countries could improve water supplies by installing similar potable water and sewerage infrastructure. Indeed, until recently, the U.S. approach to water development had been a model for other countries.

The United States and other industrial countries, however, increasingly face their own threats to freshwater resources. Peter Gleick and other water experts at the Pacific Institute for Studies in Development, Environment, and Security have noted that the United States faces tremendous water problems despite being a world leader in spending for some of the world's largest dams, irrigation systems, piped drinking water systems, and wastewater treatment plants (Gleick 2004). Installing advanced water infrastructure may have allowed the government to deliver greater amounts of better quality water to its citizens, but water development has also had unintended negative consequences. Specifically, a growing number of areas now experience periodic water shortages and dangerous forms of environmental degradation. Major rivers, such as the Hudson, Ohio, Mississippi, Missouri, Colorado, and Rio Grande, have been dammed and polluted, which has drastically altered vital freshwater ecosystems. Lakes, ponds, marshes, and other wetlands have become dumping areas for polluted water or drained to provide more land for houses, businesses, and parking lots. Ninety-five percent of the United States' fresh water is underground, but many aquifers have been overexploited. Some aquifers have become depleted and polluted to the extent that communities have been forced to close wells and transport clean water from distant areas (Kirby 2004). Such is the case with New York City's water supply, which depends on water sources further north. It is an environmental paradox that the city's overconsumption of clean fresh water has created environmental conditions that are degrading aquifers and surface water sources in distant counties north of the city (Goldstein and Izeman 1990). In other coastal areas, such as in Florida, subsidence and saltwater intrusion have significantly harmed aquifers. Many beaches and wetlands have become dumping grounds for polluted wastewater and storm water.

News accounts, books, and films reveal the consequences of pollution and overconsumption of water in the U.S. The public has been alarmed by the toxic pollution in Love Canal, New York; childhood leukemia in Massachusetts, as recounted in the book and film *A Civil Action*; and the cancer and birth defects associated with contaminated groundwater supplies in California, as portrayed in the film *Erin Brochovich*. Concerns about water quality have also led more people to consume bottled water, even though studies indicate that most brands are as pure or less pure than tap water. In 1999, people in the United States consumed over 4.5 billion gallons of bottled water at a cost of nearly $5 billion (Gleick et al. 2002, 12). As we gulp down our bottled water, it seems to me that the typical do-not-drink-the-water joke sounds less humorous now that it applies to many areas north of the U.S.–Mexico border.

In addition to degraded water quality, we increasingly deal with droughts and water shortages as well as the need for stricter water conservation measures. In arid and semiarid western regions, many cities depend on limited water supplies. For decades, the seven states that share Colorado River water with Mexico have been engaged in intense legal conflicts about how to allocate and use the limited river water (Hundley 2001). Although Los Angeles, San Diego, and other parts of southern California face water shortages, the average household continues to use 400 to 800 gallons of water per day and 30 to 40 percent of that water is used to maintain lawns in a desert ecology. Farmers grow rice, alfalfa, cotton, and other water-intensive crops in arid areas of the southwest. *Cadillac desert* seems like a fitting term when referring to the expensive and water-intensive approach to producing such crops in the American West (Reisner 1986).

In the central plains, the Ogallala aquifer stretches from South Dakota to Texas, making it North America's largest aquifer. The groundwater from the aquifer is being extracted at an alarming rate of billions of gallons each year, equivalent to over 18 times the annual flow of the Colorado River. States along the eastern coast, from Maine to Georgia, have increasingly reported droughts and, in 2002, New York City, the nation's largest city, and other East Coast cities declared drought emergencies. States in the Great Lakes region increasingly deal with water pollution as well as threats to transfer lake water to other areas, including other countries. Southern states also face problems associated with water scarcity. Florida, for example, suffers from overconsumption of ground-water, saltwater infiltration of coastal aquifers, and the ground sinking and form-ing dangerous sinkholes. During the drought of 2000, much of the Southeast watched crops die and landscapes turn brown, Florida cities put restrictions on water as wells were tapped dry and enormous sinkholes opened up due to severe subsidence of aquifers. In 2001, authorities in the Tampa Bay area declared a water emergency and restricted water use for watering lawns, washing cars, and filling fountains. Overpumping of the Tampa water supply will lead to further degradation of the aquifer, which will result in attempts to pull water from other areas. On the eastern side of the state, officials permitted diversion of water from Lake Okeechobee in 2003 to replenish coastal aquifers for the first time when Florida was not in a drought. These sorts of problems are leading to greater sup-port of expensive efforts to treat and use salty marsh water. The United States has a giant thirst that is becoming more difficult to quench (Gleick 2004; Glennon 2002; Hundley 2001; Maas and Anderson 1978; Reisner 1986).

To date, it remains too costly to convert saltwater to fresh water and trans-port the treated water across great distances. State and federal agencies have been prohibiting the construction of new dams and water reservoirs because of the environmental impact associated with these projects. The federal government has also intensified international negotiations about the Colorado River, the Rio Grande, the Great Lakes, and other bodies of water the United States shares with Canada and Mexico. These better-known examples of water problems represent issues more U.S. residents are facing on a yearly basis. As a result, the world can no longer point to the United States as a model for how to supply citizens with safe and adequate domestic water supplies. And U.S. citi-zens can no longer hold on to their assumptions that improved technology and better economic policies will address water scarcity.

NEW VISIONS OF WATER

Since the 1960s, reports have documented these harmful water use patterns. Decades of scientific study and policy debates have focused attention on the looming water crisis and the need to consider solutions. In 1992, more than 500 representatives from 100 countries reached international consensus on the water crisis at the International Conference on Water and the Environment in Dublin,

TABLE 2.1   DUBLIN PRINCIPLES

No. 1—Fresh water is a finite and vulnerable resource, essential to sustain life, development, and the environment.

No. 2—Water development and management should be based on a participatory approach, involving users, planners, and policy-makers at all levels.

No. 3—Women play a central role in the provision, management, and safeguarding of water.

No. 4—Water has an economic value in all its competing uses and should be recognized as an economic good.

Source: United Nations 1992.

Ireland. They adopted the Dublin Statement on Water and Sustainable Development, which identifies the immediate and future threats to freshwater supplies (see Table 2.1). The statement emphasizes four basic principles that ought to guide local, national, and international efforts to address the water crisis. The four principles emphasize that vital water resources are threatened and should be managed in a manner that is economically and socially comprehensive, participatory, and environmentally sound. This holistic approach is referred to as Integrated Water Resources Management (IWRM) (Inter-American Development Bank 1998; Gleick 2004). The international community has adopted the Dublin Statement, which has guided subsequent strategies of governments as well as leading international health and development organizations responsible for water resources management.

With wide recognition of a worldwide water crisis, the international community has called for a drastic shift away from extractive water development strategies. Extractive strategies tended to focus predominately on improving the engineering aspects of water projects to increase water supply for current uses as well as projected increased demands. Programs also tended to be fragmented: for example, one project might have focused on increasing the amount of groundwater pumped to a city, whereas another project focused on building a dam to increase water supply for an irrigation system. Each project, however, went forward without considering other uses of the same water resources or that the supply might not cover projected increased demands. An emphasis on technical issues fails to incorporate the participation of all stakeholders or consider long-term economic and environmental impacts of installing water infrastructure and increasing extraction of surface water and groundwater. Put more simply, the goal for too long has been to extract and supply as much water as possible without regard to indications that aquifers are not being replenished at the same rate as the extraction.

An extractive development strategy only works in settings with relatively abundant water resources and little competition over water quality and quantity. Such settings are increasingly rare. In most cases, water consumption exceeds supply so that an extractive development strategy intensifies overconsumption, pollution, shortages, and social conflict. Indeed, under current conditions, extractive water development practices have become destructive and unsustainable. The situation is serious, so we need to improve the efficiency of water use and secure adequate clean water supplies for domestic use and food production as well as to protect the environment and provide for industry (Gleick et al. 2001).

While calling for a shift away from extractive water development and over-consumption, the international community supports new integrated water management approaches. In this new perspective, greater effort is made to integrate technical aspects of water management with social, economic, and environmental aspects. Most centrally, new approaches recognize the basic right of all human beings to have access to clean water and sanitation at an affordable price. Integrated approaches recognize that the world's freshwater supply is a finite and vulnerable resource, essential to sustain life, development, and the environment. In other words, water use can no longer be guided simply by using new technology to maximize water supply for one or more specific uses. Integrated strategies take into account the need to conserve and protect freshwater supplies in a particular environmental setting. Integrated management implies finding better ways to resolve conflicts among competing uses of water and incorporate community participation and involve all users, including women, in all phases of the planning, decision-making, and allocation of water resources. Integrated approaches also call for better understanding of the cultural and social dimensions of drinking water management and for greater recognition of water's economic and social value to curb waste and inequality and increase conservation and protection of freshwater ecosystems (Gleick 2000; 2003).

Sustainability is a central aspect of integrated water management approaches. In general terms, sustainability consists of an ongoing process of creating institutions that will allow a resource to be available to future generations. Peter Gleick defines sustainable water use as "the use of water that supports the ability of human society to endure and flourish into the indefinite future without undermining the integrity of the hydrologic cycle or the ecological systems that depend on it" (2000, 131). Developing sustainable water institutions requires a long-term vision and involves experimentation, adaptation, learning, and refinement of water management. Anthropological perspectives help shed light on the social and cultural aspects of sustainable water development.

ANTHROPOLOGICAL PERSPECTIVES ON DRINKING WATER

Community participation is a central aspect of integrated water resources management approaches. Anthropologists can help identify social and cultural factors that enhance community participation and strengthen the long-term success of drinking water management in developing countries. Mary Elmendorf (1981), an anthropologist who has studied water issues in Mexico and elsewhere, argues that cultural factors need to be considered to understand why many community-based drinking water and sanitation systems in developing countries become inoperable within five years. Installing pumps and water pipes may increase the quantity of clean water delivered to individual households, but new water technology provides little benefit if water management programs overlook cultural and economic factors. An effective domestic water system depends on local control and community participation to plan and construct culturally appropriate water

Figure 2.5 Community-based drinking water projects are affected by local concerns about water quality, water quantity, and water distribution.

allocation schedules, set and collect user fees, resolve local disputes in a just manner, and coordinate labor requirements for repair, maintenance, and operation (Cox and Annis 1988; Elmendorf 1981). Local values, traditions, and customs affect many of these aspects of local water management.

Although the international community has called for more support for community participation in water development, less information exists about how to implement community-based strategies. In this case study, I examine three main issues that affect community water management: quality, quantity, and distribution (see Figure 2.5). Later chapters show how los Purifiqueños balance concerns about water quality with equally pressing concerns about how to ensure an adequate and fair distribution of scarce water.

Building on research in medical anthropology and environmental anthropology, this ethnographic study of La Purificación shows how social and cultural issues affect community-based potable water management strategies. Medical anthropology focuses on the study of human experience of health and illness across cultures, and environmental anthropology examines human experiences in relation to the environment. Both subfields of anthropology focus on the meanings and practices that groups create in relation to health and the environment, and both subfields have drawn greater attention to the impacts of political and economic forces on human health and the environment. In fact, a synthesis of the subfields has lead to a critical anthropology of environmental health, which consists of a broad set of perspectives that guide my study (Baer et al. 2003; Ennis-McMillan 1998, 2001a, 2001b; Farmer 1999; Harper 2002; Kottak 1999; Johnston and Donahue 1998; Joralemon 1999; Scheper-Hughes 1992; Whiteford 1997; Whiteford and Whiteford 2005).

Water Quality

Medical anthropology perspectives examine water quality issues beyond simply measuring chemicals and pathogens in water. Medical anthropologists have shown how culture influences the way communities conceive of and deal with water quality issues (Paul 1977). For instance, a classic study among poor families in Peru demonstrates that international health programs need to realize that local views of water quality and water-related diseases affect community participation in public health programs promoting water boiling and other water purification measures (Wellin 1955). Likewise, research in South Asia on water pollution and diarrhea shows that international health programs need to be aware that the recognition and treatment of water-related health issues vary across cultures. For instance, religious views of the sacred Ganges River in India conflict with scientific and government efforts to reduce wastewater pollution and water-related diseases (Alley 1994, 2002). In Sri Lanka public health messages about boiling water to prevent diarrhea are understood in relation to local interpretations about water quality and religious and traditional medical beliefs about eating while sick (Nichter 1985, 1988). In Brazil, cultural and religious beliefs about the afterlife need to be addressed to improve women's participation in Oral Rehydration Therapy (ORT) programs aimed at preventing infant and child death from diarrhea (Nations and Rebhun 1988). Research on dengue fever control in the Dominican Republic shows how local views of disease patterns, water storage, gender relations, and insect ecology influence community participation in prevention efforts (Whiteford 1997). These sorts of anthropology studies show that cultural interpretations of drinking water and health affect participation in community efforts to address water-related health problems. Dealing with water quality requires recognizing a variety of cultural factors.

Water Quantity

Anthropology research also shows that individuals and communities place a great deal of importance on obtaining reliable quantities of domestic water. Although we know that health status relates to good water quality, we also need to keep in mind that water scarcity has serious health consequences. Insufficient domestic water supplies increase the risk of suffering from chronic thirst, exhaustion, anxiety, lack of hygiene, and infectious diseases. Examining water quantity issues brings to light the political and economic factors that limit the poor from obtaining this vital resource. For instance, families living in poor urban settings of the Valley of Mexico suffer from constant worry about the lack of water and the economic and emotional hardship of searching for affordable domestic water supplies (García Lascuráin 1995). Limited water also means people cannot follow preventative hygiene measures, a situation that puts people at risk for cholera, skin and eye infections, and other health problems (Joralemon 1999; Juan et al. 1995). Anthropologists have also noted that in many cultures, women in particular spend considerable time and money ensuring that their households have adequate domestic water supplies (Bennett 2005; Elmendorf 1981; Ennis-McMillan 2005). Women often carry, store, and ration water, which under conditions of long-term water scarcity, create chronic stress and anxiety. Studies in water-poor areas show how people value water as an essential resource even if the water may not be suitable for drinking. In such situations, educating people about water quality may be more effective if water development programs also address people's other concerns about lack of water for bathing, doing laundry, preparing food, and other essential activities.

Water Distribution

Environmental anthropologists also show how local culture shapes the distribution and use of natural resources. As water becomes more scarce, it becomes economically and socially more valuable. Communities, however, distribute water in a variety of ways. Residents of the United States and other industrial countries are often accustomed to water distribution systems that treat water as a commodity that can be bought and sold. Individuals and corporations with more wealth pay the cost of consuming water and discharging wastewater. Many communities criticize this view because it emphasizes competition and profit seeking, which encourages overconsumption of water rather than conservation of water and has led to water shortages and unequal distribution. Within some communities, clean water is often distributed to some parts of society—such as wealthier neighborhoods and agribusiness—even though other segments of society live with shortages. For instance, poor shantytown residents in Brazil express their thirst and struggle for water in relation to social inequalities and political factors that channel water to wealthier groups (Scheper-Hughes 1992). Indeed, such research suggests that water and sanitation programs might be more successful if they incorporate cultural beliefs but also an awareness of the social inequalities that limit distribution of water to certain populations.

In contrast to dominant practices of industrial and capitalist societies, many traditional communities view water as a communal resource that ought to be distributed in an equitable fashion to members of the community that fulfill traditional obligations. This egalitarian form of distribution is most apparent in environmental anthropology research on irrigation management. Studies throughout Latin America show how communities distribute water in ways that allow the entire community to benefit (Enge and Whiteford 1989; Guillet 1992; Guillet and Mitchell 1994; Palerm Viqueira 1995; Whiteford and Bernal 1996; Whiteford and Melville 2002). Communities maintain local control of water resources and develop ways to counter more powerful groups that seek to divert limited freshwater supplies to particular sectors. Because cultural values shape notions of equity and justice, anthropologists can offer valuable insight into mechanisms that ensure a fair distribution and use of water. Enge and Whiteford's work in Mexico (1989) and Guillet's work in Peru (1992) document how communities define water as a common property of the community rather than private property for sale on an open market. Such communities develop local customs for reinforcing a cohesive and cooperative social network to ensure a fair distribution of water. Communities also often have traditional ways of allocating water and resolving conflicts, promoting conservation, and maintaining the water system (Johnston and Donahue 1998). Overall, this research suggests that traditional water distribution practices may reduce water-related suffering in some areas.

CONCLUSION

La Purificación's location on the edge of a water crisis challenges us to reflect on how each of us lives on the edge of a worldwide freshwater crisis. International efforts to invest in new water infrastructure and the latest water technology have not solved the water crisis, and, instead, have intensified over-consumption, inefficient water use, pollution, inequitable resource distribution, poverty, water shortages, social conflicts, and environmental degradation. As a result, human health and environmental sustainability are threatened.

Recent international efforts have shifted from destructive water development to integrated water resources management, which takes a more comprehensive approach to protecting precious water resources. Efforts to promote community participation in integrated approaches require better understanding of the cultural aspects of the water users. Anthropological perspectives can be useful for identifying traditional practices, resources, and institutions associated with effective community-based drinking water management strategies. To design sustainable water systems, we need to consider local views that balance concerns for drinking water quality with equally pressing concerns about water quantity, user rights and responsibilities, proper infrastructure, and equitable resource distribution. La Purificación's case demonstrates how people use culture to address some of the difficult challenges of sustaining community participation in drinking water management. By examining how los Purifiqueños understand the interrelationship between quality, quantity, and distribution, this ethnographic study demonstrates how anthropological perspective can contribute to international efforts to improve community participation in drinking water management.

3/"The Soul of a Pueblo"
Local Water History

After completing exploratory research in the summer of 1993, I returned to Michigan and designed a larger ethnographic project on water management in La Purificación. In December 1994, I returned to Mexico to conduct research in La Purificación for 18 months. I was fortunate to be able to find housing with Amelia and her mother, Sarita, the same women with whom I lived during the summer of 1993. At that time, Amelia was in her sixties and Sarita was in her nineties, and they lived together in a small one-bedroom, cement-block house. They allowed me to rent a similar small house located a few feet away from their house, and they adopted me into their family. I became Amelia's nephew and Sarita's grandson. Sarita was born in La Purificación in 1903, so when I met her, she was quite elderly and did not leave the house much. Sarita was hard of hearing and partially blind with cataracts, and her hands were knotted with arthritis. She had beautiful snow-white hair and often sat at the dining table petting Mursi, her little Chihuahua. Because she stayed at home most of the time, Sarita had a lot of time to talk. We often spent part of each day visiting with one another.

Sarita always had a story to tell and especially delighted in telling me what she knew about the history and customs of the region. I got in the habit of taking notes during our visits and tape-recorded several conversations. Sarita recounted that in the area where La Purificación is now located, the indigenous rulers of Texcoco constructed a beautiful garden hundreds of years before the Spaniards came. She also described how her relatives worked on the nearby haciendas in the small agricultural community she remembered before the Mexican Revolution. She also remembered the violence of the revolution, which broke out in 1910. She recounted how, as a little girl, her family hid her in a well to protect her from the armed conflict. After both of her parents died in the 1920s, Sarita lived with relatives in Mexico City and worked as a domestic servant for several families. Later, she married Guillermo who also had moved from La Purificación to Mexico City, and they raised six children. In the 1970s, they bought a piece of property from

Figure 3.1 Sitting with my Mexican family. Sarita (left) and Amelia (right) and their pet Chihuahuas lived in this one-bedroom house, and I rented the small house next door.

Sarita's cousin in La Purificación and built the one-bedroom house as a weekend getaway from Mexico City. After Guillermo died, Sarita moved back to her native village.

Amelia, Sarita's third child, was born and raised in Mexico City, but as a girl she often visited La Purificación with her parents. She never married and did not have children. In her fifties, she became frustrated with her secretarial job at a publishing company and tired of the stress and strain of living in Mexico City. Amelia retired and moved to La Purificación and built the small house next to her mother. Amelia is a little taller than her mother, and her dark hair now has streaks of gray. Her skin is brown from spending time gardening, and when I lived there she often rode about town in her white Volkswagen Beetle, visiting friends with Mursi sitting on her shoulders. When I arrived, Amelia was living with her mother and taking care of her. The two women depended on the rent from Amelia's house to supplement their small income from Amelia's retirement pension and Sarita's social security.

Living with Amelia and Sarita gave me a wonderful opportunity to learn about the history of the community and understand the changes from the perspective of local residents. In the following sections, I present a brief history—shaped by interactions and oral history interviews with residents—of La Purificación. The history focuses on the importance of water in local life and shows the longstanding custom of viewing water as a common resource managed for the benefit of the entire community.

A HIDDEN HISTORY

La Purificación's current form of managing drinking water supplies has a long but, in some ways, hidden history. The community began installing the electric pumps, metal water pipes, and stone water tanks in the late 1970s, but the local principles and practices for dealing with water rights and responsibilities are rooted in traditions that extend across centuries. This chapter provides an overview of the historical context of water control in La Purificación. Some information about the regional history appears in books, but I gathered much of La Purificación's water history from oral histories and from documents tucked away in the community's civil offices (Ennis-McMillan 1998). This information shows how a system for channeling mountain springwater through dirt and stone irrigation canals provided the foundation for the contemporary system for piping groundwater primarily for household purposes. For centuries, water has been a central aspect of community life, one that people regard as *el alma del pueblo* or "the soul of the pueblo."[1]

Piecing together La Purificación's local water history helped me understand, for example, why los Purifiqueños view water as a collective resource and why they connect drinking water with religious fiestas. Part of the explanation relates to the idea that an individual's access to water—for irrigation or household purposes—carries the obligation of working for the benefit of the community. Sometimes people work directly with the water system, but sometimes people provide labor for other purposes, including for religious festivals. That is the custom, residents told me. Water for household use has always been a concern, but, until recently, its importance was overshadowed by the greater importance of irrigation water to grow food and commercial crops. It might seem to outsiders that the modern-looking drinking water system has replaced the traditional canal system. Taking a closer look, however, one can see that the current drinking water system builds on a deep history of irrigation traditions and practices.

NORTHERN ACOLHUACAN: AN INDIGENOUS HERITAGE

La Purificación is located in the foothills that form part of a larger region anthropologists refer to as northern Acolhuacan. The region is bounded by extensions of the Sierra Nevada Mountains to the east, and by Lake Texcoco to the west. Water melting from sierra snowpacks feeds a series of mountain springs, which, in turn, empty into several rivers that course down the mountains and foothills and eventually drain into Lake Texcoco. Until the fifteenth century, people in the region lived in scattered communities near the rivers and the lake. Relying on foraging and small-scale agriculture, small independent settlements remained on the outskirts of the larger indigenous empires that emerged elsewhere in the Valley of Mexico.

Northern Acolhuacan takes its name from the fifteenth-century Acolhua State whose administrative center was located in the city of Texcoco on the eastern

---

[1]The word *pueblo* means both the people and the community.

Figure 3.2 Statue of Netzahualcóyotl in present-day Texcoco.

shores of Lake Texcoco. In the fifteenth century, communities from the sierra and the valley floor were united into an economic, political, and religious network that eventually formed the Acolhua State. Rulers of the state included the famous poet-king Netzahualcóyotl. The Acolhua State later joined the Mexica State ruled from Tenochtitlan to form part of the Triple Alliance that ruled the Aztec Empire. The Aztecs, led by the Mexica, controlled much of the territory that now falls within the central and southern parts of present-day Mexico (Berdan 2005). Like the majority of the inhabitants of the empire, the northern Acolhua people lived in settled communities, relied on intensive agriculture, and spoke Nahuatl.

The Acolhua State gained control over the region's land and water resources stretching from the sierras to Lake Texcoco (McAfee and Barlow 1946; Palerm Viqueira 1995; Wolf and Palerm 1955). The centralized control of sierra springs accounted for an important source of Netzahualcóyotl's power. Water was an essential agricultural resource for developing this large-scale society, but water was also necessary for domestic purposes. The Acolhua regime expanded and elaborated an extensive canal system in the region, using innovative technological features not found in other parts of the world at that time (Doolittle 1990). The canal system tapped abundant surface water supplies from the springs located at colder, higher elevations of the sierra. Canals made of dirt and stone channeled the water to the foothills and fertile valley floor where warmer temperatures allowed people to raise food crops, principally maize, squash, and beans. Communities at lower elevations benefited from an increased supply of water for irrigating crops before the rainy season, which increased the crop yield before the onset of winter frost. Communities at cooler, higher elevations near the mountain springs exchanged a portion of their water to obtain food supplies produced by communities at lower and warmer elevations.

The Acolhua rulers mobilized a tremendous amount of labor to build and maintain the elaborate hydraulic system. The centralized authority obligated people to provide labor outside their communities for regional water projects in exchange for access to water, which rulers granted for both agricultural production and household use. The increased agricultural production provided food for denser urban settlements and supported political and religious leaders, military specialists, artisans, and other nonfood-producing occupants. Furthermore, the regional administration of water reinforced a cohesive social organization, integrated communities across different ecological areas, and shaped occupational specialties and regional trading patterns. Netzahualcóyotl and other Acolhua rulers granted water rights to communities, not individuals, which reflected the prevalent indigenous notion that water was a communal resource rather than an individually held resource.

Although no settlements existed in the foothills during the pre-Hispanic era, Acolhua communities from lower elevations used the foothills for agricultural production. One segment of the region's hydraulic system channeled the mountain springwater to create terraced gardens in the small valley where La Purificación is presently located. Netzahualcóyotl oversaw the construction of baths and terraces that allowed water to cascade down the hillsides of

Figure 3.3 Teztcutzingo. The small hill to the right is called Teztcutzingo and is a national historic site preserving archaeological ruins of water canals, baths, and gardens built during Netzahualcóyotl's reign. This view is from a high point in La Purificación.

Figure 3.4 Celebrating mass in La Purificación's Catholic church.

Tetzcutzingo and form part of a garden for plants and animals collected from distant areas throughout the Aztec Empire.

Today, visitors can see terraced hillsides and find remnants of the indigenous canal system throughout the area. La Purificación and several other communities rely on surface water that travels through a remaining part of the indigenous canal system. Terraces and an unused portion of the canals are visible within La Purificación, and tourists regularly visit the archaeological site at Tetzcutzingo.

SPANISH CONQUEST AND COLONIZATION

The sixteenth-century Spanish Conquest and subsequent colonization brought a new political, economic, and cultural order to the Nahuatl-speaking people of northern Acolhuacan. The Spanish took over Texcoco and used the city as their administrative center. They also took over the fertile land in the valley floor and established large haciendas for growing wheat, raising sheep, and producing other agricultural goods. Colonial administrators took control of the regional water system and channeled surface water away from indigenous settlements to irrigate the colonists' agricultural land and provide power for the mills for processing wheat and wool. The Spanish rulers forced indigenous people to provide food crops and other tribute to the colonists and labor for the large landowners. Colonists also imposed Roman Catholicism on the Indians and installed churches and chapels in cities and Indian pueblos. Indigenous settlements in the plains diminished when residents were displaced by large landowners or died from exposure to Old World diseases. Some indigenous people migrated to the unoccupied and less desirable foothills and made a living by combining subsistence agriculture with labor on nearby haciendas and mills.

La Purificación was one of a series of Indian pueblos that emerged in the foothills on marginal strips of rocky land with limited water supplies. The pueblo relied on the pre-Hispanic canals that supplied the sierra springwater for irrigation, but the settlement's survival also depended on using this same water for drinking, cooking, bathing, and other basic necessities. According to local accounts, the first settlers of La Purificación came from La Asunción, a pueblo located in the valley floor. Legend has it that when plagues ravaged the area and haciendas took over people's land, people from La Asunción migrated to the foothills to escape sickness and death. The new site was supposed to be purified of disease. When the settlers founded a Roman Catholic church in the seventeenth century, they chose as its religious patron La Virgen de la Candelaria, representing the purification of the Virgin Mary. The fiesta of February 2 celebrates the day when Mary, following Jewish custom at the time, went to the temple 40 days after giving birth to present her newborn child and complete a purification ceremony. Images of the Virgin Mary show her carrying the newborn Christ in one arm and holding a candle in the other. The community eventually became known as La Purificación Tepetitla. Names of northern Acolhuacan communities typically consist of a Roman Catholic saint or virgin followed by a Nahuatl place name. In this case, La Purificación refers to the community's patron virgin, and *Tepetitla* is a Nahuatl word that means under or at the base of the hills, referring to the pueblo's location in a small valley surrounded by several hills.

In the eighteenth century, La Purificación's few hundred residents fought outside threats to the community's small but vital allocation of surface water that flowed in the old canals. The water eventually emptied into a nearby small river that led to a hacienda called Molino de Flores. Like most of the region's haciendas, the Spanish owners took control of nearby land, water, and other natural resources for agricultural production. La Purificación and other small communities surrounding the hacienda constantly struggled with the Molino de Flores to maintain a modest but necessary portion of this water. The hacienda relied on the residents of these pueblos as a cheap source of labor and allowed the pueblos to have enough water to satisfy basic needs, but all surplus water was channeled to the hacienda for use in producing agricultural goods. Water nourished the hacienda animals, powered the mills for grinding wheat and corn, and provided an essential ingredient for producing *pulque,* a locally produced alcohol made from century plants. This ongoing struggle between pueblos and the haciendas illustrates how water was often channeled to more powerful social groups who used the water for economic gain rather than basic needs.

Figure 3.5 Visiting the old hacienda, Molino de Flores.

The Indian pueblos lost control of water for growing food and for household necessities.

Eventually, the Spanish Crown intervened in the conflict. In 1757, a locally appointed Spanish official petitioned the Spanish viceroy for La Purificación's continued rights to the canal water, claiming that irrigation for local gardens and orchards was essential for the continued existence of the pueblo. Colonial documents refer to residents of La Purificación as Indians. Nevertheless, like residents of other indigenous communities, Los Purifiqueños were becoming assimilated into the dominant Spanish–Catholic society. Against the wishes of neighboring Indian pueblos and large landholders, the Spanish rulers granted La Purificación rights to a portion of the water. The Spanish Crown routinely granted communal land and water rights to Indian pueblos to support tribute-paying subjects. The Crown also sought to limit large landowners from controlling valuable natural resources and thus gaining power to challenge the Crown's authority. Today, officials in La Purificación guard a copy of the 1757 water grant as valuable proof of the community's longstanding water claims.

MEXICAN INDEPENDENCE

Mexico declared independence from Spain in 1810 and gained formal independence by 1821. Without the Spanish Crown's intervention, the haciendas in northern Acolhuacan and elsewhere expanded their control over water resources as well as agricultural land, pastures, and forests. Indian pueblo rights were taken away and most rural people—both indigenous and nonindigenous—were simply referred to as *campesinos. Campesino* is the Spanish term for peasant, which is a small-scale agriculturalist who relies on subsistence crops. They also rely on other economic activities, such as sale of produce, wage labor, and craft production, which allows them to pay rent to landlords and satisfy government obligations, including paying taxes. Although campesinos live in small agricultural communities and abide by local customs, they also live in state-organized societies and must abide by government laws. During the nineteenth century, La Purificación and other foothill communities lost portions of surface water allocated during colonial times. The Hacienda de Chapingo and Molino de Flores were two of the larger operations in northern Acolhuacan, but owners of numerous other haciendas, mills, and ranches gained greater control over local land and water resources. Many people in the pueblos continued to combine subsistence agriculture with labor on haciendas and mills. These economic changes and population increases intensified competition for limited water supplies.

Despite competing claims on the water resources, La Purificación maintained access to a portion of the surface water. Residents, however, remained concerned about securing more water and frequently requested support from officials in Texcoco to construct a better dam to store greater volumes of water. Residents from La Purificación worked on the haciendas, and most households possessed individual plots to cultivate food crops as well as gardens called *huertas* for growing fruit, flowers, and medicinal plants for household use and for sale in urban markets. Community authorities allocated the water for both irrigation and household use. Community residents received water for irrigation and household use if they contributed water fees and provided mandatory unpaid labor for public works projects and community fiestas. Because everyone benefited by receiving all of the community's resources and not just water, everyone had to work for the benefit of the community. In this way, water remained a communal resource, distributed according to local principles of equity.

REVOLUTION AND EXPANDED
SURFACE WATER RIGHTS

The 1910 Mexican Revolution brought further changes in social relations in northern Acolhuacan. During the earlier and violent phase of the revolution, banditry and fighting between revolutionary armies devastated the region and many families abandoned their homes and lands. The haciendas and mills collapsed after fighting broke out and former workers fled to look for work in Mexico City and other areas. Hunger, drought, influenza, and other diseases also took their toll as many communities become depopulated. The social conflict also destabilized the large landowners' control of land and water.

The revolution had a strong agrarian component that fought to end exploitation of campesinos by giving them land and liberty. Mexico's revolutionary unrest eventually declined and in 1917 the nation passed a new constitution that outlined, among other things, a series of agrarian reform programs expropriating land and water from haciendas and granting the resources to campesino communities. The most common form of land grant was the *ejido,* which is agricultural land held by the community in a cooperative manner. In most areas of Mexico, communities sought ways to increase their holding on land before seeking rights to more water. In La Purificación Tepetitla, however, the agrarian reform took a different course, beginning first with water and then with land.

Petitioning for Water

Unlike most areas of Mexico, many foothill and sierra communities in northern Acolhuacan took the less common strategy of petitioning the federal government for expanded access to water before petitioning for an ejido. In December 1917, shortly after the passage of the new constitution, La Purificación began a lengthy and difficult process of petitioning state and federal officials for surface water from sierra springs, which, to use the words in the documents, the community has possessed "since time immemorial." This made La Purificación one of the first communities in the region to petition for increased access to water, which numerous documents refer to as "the precious liquid" and "the soul of the pueblo."

Although stressing the importance of irrigation water, the petitions also noted that the lack of a local water source meant that the community also depended on the surface water for household needs. At this time, La Purificación had fewer than 500 inhabitants, and the community's principal means of livelihood depended on using poor-quality foothill land to cultivate various food and commercial products: wheat; fruit such as *membrillo,* avocado, pear, and *tejocote* from orchards; and several varieties of flowers and medicinal plants. Residents sold many of the products in Texcoco and Mexico City. At first, La Purificación proposed to reclaim the portion of water granted the community during the colonial period. Later, however, community officials proposed to also receive portions of water that went to Hacienda de Chapingo, Molino de Flores, and other haciendas in the plains below.

From 1917 to 1924, La Purificación sent letters to numerous government officials arguing for justice to alleviate hardships of living year after year with scarce water supplies. Such letters eloquently described the challenges of living in a semiarid foothill area with rocky and sandy soils and depending on unpredictable rains to cultivate maize and other food and commercial crops. In good years, the soil was productive, but if the rainy season started too late—as it did in many years—people harvested little more than corn stalks, which could only be used for animal feed. Officials also requested assistance to build new canals and a dam, as well as help to guard against water theft by neighboring communities. They also demanded that the authorities end the wasteful practices of downstream communities and haciendas that allowed large portions of unused river water to drain into Lake Texcoco. Better-quality and more reliable water would help provide a more secure corn harvest each year and ensure sufficient water for household uses.

On September 2, 1924, La Purificación received a document signed by President Alvaro Obregón conceding rights to a portion of the surface water that flowed from sierra springs, through old irrigation canals, and into the Río Coxcacuaco. Part of this claim was based on the 1757 document mentioned

Figure 3.6 An aguador
channels surface water
through the irrigation
canals.

previously. Before the revolution, the river had been called Río del Molino, taking its name from the El Molino de Flores that controlled the river water. After the revolution, the hacienda lost its control over its land and water and the river became officially designated Río Coxcacuaco. Portions of the water were granted to campesino communities primarily for irrigation to improve agricultural production, but a small portion was also granted for household consumption.

By 1928, La Purificación was assigned to the Río Coxcacuaco water council, an irrigation unit that at the time consisted of 12 communities and haciendas stretching from the sierra springs of San Francisco to Lake Texcoco. La Purificación obtained rights to a specific allocation of the surface water as part of the new irrigation unit, and the community has maintained this allocation since that time. The haciendas, for the most part, disappeared after the government expropriated most of the land and water resources and redistributed the resources to campesino communities. The central buildings of the former Hacienda de Chapingo became the site of the University of Chapingo, which became known for its emphasis on agricultural sciences. The buildings of the former Molino de Flores were transformed into a historical site and are quite busy with tourists on the weekends.

In 1929, five years after granting La Purificación water rights, the government granted the community an ejido consisting of land expropriated from another hacienda at a lower elevation. This land grant, however, did not include water rights, so residents produced only rain-fed crops. The community used the ejido to increase subsistence agricultural production of rain-fed crops such as maize, squash, and beans and to pasture cows, sheep, and horses. In addition, using the ejido freed up irrigated private land at higher elevations for increased commercial production of ornamental flowers, fruit trees, medicinal plants, and herbs.

By the 1940s, the new land and water resources allowed the community to intensify campesino agricultural production, but households continued to rely on wage labor and craft production. Lake Texcoco separated northern Acolhuacan from the metropolitan area of Mexico City, so the population remained relatively out of the way from the growing urban center. Residents, however, had frequent contact with the city, and many regularly traveled to sell agricultural products in city markets. The trip to Mexico City and back took an entire day and usually involved a combination of travel by foot, horse, and boat.

Water Distribution

Until the 1970s when the community installed a piped water system, La Purificación relied on the surface water for all of its needs. La Purificación's water officials managed the surface water and administered the water fees for both irrigation and household use. Most of the water was used for irrigation and a smaller portion provided the major source for the household water supply. Only a few households had separate wells that tapped small pools of water trapped in pockets of volcanic rock near the surface. Surface water was the major community resource that all community residents shared in common.

An *aguador* (water carrier) oversaw the actual distribution of the surface water. It took the aguador two weeks to deliver water to one-half of the community and then another two weeks to deliver water to the other half. In each barrio, the aguador spent most of this time delivering irrigation water to each user. After completing the irrigation schedule, the aguador took a few additional days filling each household's *jagüey,* which is a round, uncovered reservoir for storing water for household use. A jagüey is usually several yards in diameter, dug in the ground, lined with stones, and connected to a canal that channels surface water into the reservoir. Each household usually filled their jagüey once a month and relied on this water for all household needs. In this system, households stored water in each jagüey and relied on the water for a month until the aguador returned to fill the reservoir again. Without electricity for pumps, people used buckets to haul water from the jagüey to the house for drinking, bathing, cooking, and other household uses. Residents paid the aguador a fee separate from fees for irrigation water. Most households had their own jagüey, but some households shared jagüeyes with neighbors. Residents who used one of the few public jagüeyes were obligated to help clean and repair the public reservoir.

Figure 3.7 Irrigation users during a faena *to clean the irrigation canals.*

Cargos and Surface Water

Up until the 1970s, the distribution of water for household use was directly linked with the distribution of water for agricultural use. All community residents could request access to surface water, and this access obligated them to pay water fees, contribute unpaid labor to *faenas*, and accept civil and religious *cargos* when called upon. Faena is essentially corvée labor, which is obligatory, unpaid community labor usually required of residents in lieu of or in addition to taxes for drinking water projects, irrigation systems, road repair, and other public works projects. Cargos are civil or religious offices to which people are elected to serve within the local municipal government or the local Catholic church. The civil cargos consisted of 12 or so positions (the number varied with each administration). These cargos were considered the higher positions of local authority and they were responsible for overseeing particular community affairs. The religious cargos consisted of a group of eight to 10 men who were given the title of *mayordomo* and were responsible for sponsoring and organizing an annual cycle of religious fiestas. Both the civil and religious cargos were selected from married men who used surface water for irrigation. Residents who had more land and used more irrigation water were named to higher civil and religious cargos and held them more often than those who used less irrigation water.

The practice of naming irrigation users to civil and religious cargos relates to the fact that those with irrigation water benefited from the labor of others. Because all households participated in faenas to clean canals, build new canals, and repair the system, it seemed fair that irrigation users give back to the community by performing cargo service. The head of each household was obligated

Figure 3.8 Drinking Water Committee members monitor La Purificación's pump for extracting groundwater.

once a week to clean sewage drains, connections to jagüeyes, and irrigation canals, which ran in front of the household's property. Failure to complete such tasks put the household at risk for being fined by authorities. Men who held offices as mayorodomos—religious officers who organize the annual fiestas for local Catholic saints and virgins—were exempt from other forms of obligatory cooperative labor. In La Purificación, as occurred in neighboring communities, eligible men who refused to fulfill community service obligations risked being denied access to irrigation water. Because all households depended on the irrigation water for household uses, this punishment also meant a household was left without a reliable household water supply. Thus, before installing a piped water system, the community instituted a general custom that linked any water use to the fulfillment of community obligations.

An egalitarian water distribution, however, does not mean that the community was free of differences and conflict. Locally prominent families influenced the elections to fill cargos each term and sometimes name people to a series of cargos for consecutive years rather than rotating the cargos among the entire community. Wealthier families tended to occupy the highest cargos and have greater influence in local civil and religious matters. These families also obligated less wealthy families to occupy lesser civil and religious cargos. Naming somebody to consecutive cargos was done sometimes in a vindictive manner and was used by prominent families to control less wealthy households and obligate them to redistribute their wealth and labor. These sorts of issues indicate that the community was stratified, even though residents shared other cultural characteristics.

DEVELOPING GROUNDWATER SUPPLIES

Obtaining a firm right to surface water benefited La Purificación enormously in the few decades after the revolution. Up to the 1970s, La Purificación had 100 or so households and 500 to 750 residents who engaged in a combination of subsistence agriculture, small-scale commercial agriculture, and wage work. The population remained steady because residents regularly left the community in search of work and few people moved to the community. Throughout the twentieth century, the people who remained in the pueblo referred to themselves as campesinos. By the late 1960s, the community became concerned about the dwindling and polluted surface water and the ongoing conflicts with neighboring communities over the shared source of surface water. These concerns motivated local efforts to tap new underground water sources and install a piped water system.

The first efforts to develop groundwater supplies met with limited success. Geological studies in the 1950s concluded that it was nearly impossible to tap groundwater within La Purificación. A few shallow wells of 30 to 100 feet deep tapped small pools of rainwater trapped near the surface among layers of volcanic rock. Residents also collected water from a few small springs, but these too eventually ceased providing water. Electricity had been installed in the 1950s, making it possible to run an electric water pump. Geological surveys concluded that tapping abundant aquifers would require drilling through more than 1,000 feet of nearly impenetrable layers of volcanic rock, which would be too difficult and too deep to pump groundwater efficiently to the surface. During the 1960s, the community obtained limited funds from the Secretary of Health and Assistance (Secretaría de Salud y Asistencia, SSA), a federal agency that at the time coordinated public health initiatives to improve drinking water supplies in the region. La Purificación used state and federal funds to install a pump, build a water tank, and install some pipes that improved the delivery of the limited amount of groundwater that existed within the community. Without a reliable source of groundwater, this early project soon failed and left the community without a proper drinking water supply.

Later, the community requested permission and funds from the federal government to drill a well at a lower elevation in the plains where nearby communities had tapped steady underground aquifers. Engineers suggested that it would be a viable but costly option to pump groundwater from a lower elevation up to the foothills where the households were located. The SSA denied La Purificación's request. In response, the community took a creative and somewhat clandestine approach to obtaining the drinking water they so desperately needed.

A Hidden Drinking Water Project

By the 1970s, the profitability of agriculture was in decline and households placed a greater reliance on expanded opportunities in the region's industrial economy. Men and women earned wages in factories, construction, the service industry, and transportation. La Purificación and nearby foothill and sierra communities became transformed with more schools, paved roads, and better piped water. Most importantly, the population grew as more people stayed in the community and urban dwellers settled in the foothill setting. This sort of industrialization and urbanization was occurring throughout the Valley of Mexico.

An influx of cash, an increasing population, and a growing importance placed on water for nonagricultural uses influenced La Purificación's development of a piped water supply. A group of residents with new economic wealth from nonagricultural work organized a project to drill a well in the ejido and pump groundwater up to the settlement. Members of the group formed a voluntary organizing committee that invested money in the piped water project. The community supported the project, which was initially planned as a way to improve household water supplies as well as provide supplemental irrigation water for commercial greenhouse production. The new investment in greenhouses allowed people to increase cultivation of ornamental flowers, medicinal plants, and other commercial crops. In addition to developing the piped water system, the community also opened up a new road so that a private bus line could provide better transportation for people traveling to work and school and transporting their goods to Texcoco, Mexico City, and other urban markets.

All new wells in Mexico have to be registered with the federal government. La Purificación's community officials registered the water project as an irrigation well, but the community ran the well in a semi-clandestine manner as a household water supply. The community could not officially call this a drinking water project because the federal government had restricted drilling new deep wells because of the falling groundwater levels and increasing ground subsidence in the Valley of Mexico. This restriction also reflected a tendency for the federal government to provide funds to rural communities for developing irrigation systems rather than drinking water projects. Because the community could not obtain outside support to drill a deep well to improve the household water supply, it sought government support to develop an irrigation system. The surface water already supplied the community with irrigation water, so a new groundwater supply was supposed to serve as a supplemental water source. People involved in the early phases of the project said it was officially called an irrigation project, but most people assumed that the main aim of the project was to provide the community with a cleaner and more abundant supply of water for household use.

By officially calling it an irrigation project rather than a drinking water project, La Purificación received federal approval as well as agricultural subsidies to cover the installation and maintenance costs of a piped water system. The Secretary of Hydraulic Resources (Secretaría de Recursos Hidráulicos, SRH) expected the community to abide by federal guidelines for rural development programs and form an irrigation unit, which the community did. Working with elected community representatives, the project's organizing committee oversaw major aspects of the project, including drilling the well, installing a pump and pipes, hooking up electricity to run the pump, and managing faena groups. The group collected monetary contributions from irrigation users and also formed a voluntary pro-drinking water committee that collected contributions from residents who expected to use the groundwater for household purposes. As it had done with surface water, La Purificación's new piped groundwater system incorporated household water management into irrigation management. In contrast to earlier efforts, however, the water for household use took a higher priority than irrigation water.

The new well began functioning in 1976 with a powerful water pump, which an engineer designed especially for the well. The engineer, who lived hundreds of miles away in the state of Guanajato, told organizers that at that time they probably had the most powerful water pump in the Valley of Mexico. Apparently, no other setting needed such a forceful water pump, because communities at lower elevations easily pumped groundwater to the surface and communities at higher elevations used gravity to channel mountain springwater to their properties. Up to the 1980s, La Purificación's new system functioned well and the community expanded the network of water pipes, connected more households to the system, and built two additional water tanks.

Out in the Open

In the mid-1980s, the piped water system began having its first set of major problems. The aging pump began to wear out and break down. Further, the groundwater table was falling, so the failing pump had to work harder to draw water to the surface. More demand was also placed on the system because the population of about 2,000 people more than doubled from a decade earlier. Now that the community had electricity, better schools, improved roads and transportation service, and, of course, piped water, fewer people left the community and more people from urban areas began purchasing property and building new houses in this foothill setting. Organizers of the piped water project had assumed that the well would provide enough water to supplement surface water for both irrigation and household use. Mechanical problems with the system, however, led the community to reserve groundwater for domestic purposes and prohibit its use for irrigation, including greenhouse production.

In 1988, La Purificación began officially managing the drinking water system independent from the irrigation system. The community reached an agreement with the State of Mexico to drill a new drinking water well. Although the government prohibited communities from drilling new wells in the region, La Purificación's new well was permitted because it was a relocation of a previous well. Federal, state, municipio, and community authorities assisted with various facets of the project, and officials from the Institutional Revolutionary Party (Partido Revolucionario Institucional, PRI) acted as intermediaries between the community and other government officials regarding requests for construction materials and technical assistance. In contrast to other projects, this water project explicitly used funds, technical expertise, and materials to improve the drinking water supply rather than develop the irrigation system. These changes signaled a new prominence of the household water system over the irrigation.

The project resulted in the drilling of a deep well to tap an aquifer located at a depth of about 450 feet, which allowed the water to rise up the well to about 225 to 250 feet from the ground. After the new well was drilled, community authorities wrote to federal and state officials for several years before obtaining the balance of funds to complete the project. The community needed funds to purchase large water pipes, test and register the new well, install a pump, and connect the electricity. A combination of technical problems and the demands created by a population that was approaching 3,000 people led authorities to increase water fees and reduce water delivery to each household to about four hours a day.

By 1994, the community obtained the necessary resources to complete other phases of the project, including the installation of a 250-horsepower water pump that easily channeled water through the system. In the end, La Purificación received assistance from several government agencies, including the SSA, the State Commission of Water and Sanitation (Comisión Estatal de Agua y Saneamiento, CEAS), and the Secretary for Urban Development and Ecology (Secretaría de Desarrollo Urbano y Ecología, SEDUE). Funds and technical support from the municipio of Texcoco and the National Solidarity Program (Programa Nacional de Solidaridad) supported the final phases of the project, including the connection of the electricity to the water pump. During this process, the electric company was notified that the water from the well was for domestic purposes, which brought an end to some of the rural subsidies for electric power and raised the cost of managing the piped water system.

At the beginning of the 1994–1996 administration of civil authorities, the new well was ready to supply the population, which had grown to over 4,000 people. The system was more efficient, but it also had higher maintenance and repair costs. At a community assembly, residents approved a resolution authorizing the Drinking Water Committee to collect a one-time contribution of 110 pesos from each of the 605 households with registered water connections. The community also increased monthly water fees from 10 pesos to 25 pesos and limited the water delivery schedule to a few hours every other day. It was left up to each household to store water in their own reservoirs for use at a later time. By the time I arrived to conduct research in December 1994, this well supplied most households with piped water for drinking and other basic necessities. Few households, if any, used the surface water for other household purposes. The community further expanded the network of pipes and added a fourth water tank. In 1996, 865 registered household had water connections. By 2003 the community had grown to nearly 6,000 people, and officials reported nearly 1,200 household water connections.

Reorganizing the Cargos

Changes in La Purificación's administration of water resources affected the community's organization of civil and religious cargos. Almost all households have a registered household water connection to the piped groundwater system, but fewer than 270 households receive surface water, which they use almost exclusively for irrigation. With each decade, fewer residents rely on agriculture and have less need for irrigation.

In terms of civil cargos, the community phased out the voluntary water committee and formally established a permanent elected Drinking Water Committee, which added seven new civil cargos to the *delegación*. This change from a voluntary to a permanent committee formally incorporated drinking water management into the duties of elected civil officials and signaled the growing importance of piped water for household use. Like all cargos, the new drinking water cargos are supposed to be rotated among all households in the community. People who are elected to the Drinking Water Committee, however, have tended to be established male residents with ties to agriculture, whether they are *ejidatarios,* owners of privately owned irrigated land, or both. Many cargo holders have tended to be from upper and middle socioeconomic strata of the community and engage in some form of commercial agriculture. In this manner, drinking water authorities have tended to represent the interests of established residents who identify themselves as campesinos. This process also means people familiar with the technical and cultural aspects of managing surface water also manage the new groundwater system.

Similarly, religious cargos were reorganized and required fiesta sponsorship from all property owners—both men and women—rather than simply men with irrigation water. For annual elections, office holders are drawn from the list of male and female property owners, usually referred to as the heads of the household. By the 1980s, new people began occupying religious cargos, including women elected to the festival organizing groups, called the mayordomías. Women began being elected as members of the groups and carried the title *mayordoma.* Some women were elected *fiscalas,* the title used for the head of the mayordomías. New types of participants in the cargo system included new residents and members of households who do not use irrigation water. In addition, in a few cases, non-Catholics were elected and served in the mayordomías. Refusal to accept a religious cargo has resulted in a number of penalties, including denying permission to use the church for weddings, baptisms, funerals, and other important life-cycle ceremonies. Religious authorities sometimes ask civil authorities to also deny a family burial rights in the local cemetery. In more severe cases, religious officials request civil officials to impose the harshest penalty: shutting off a household's piped water supply. These cases illustrate the persistence of long-standing principles of water management. In particular, water is a communal resource and access to water obligates residents to fulfill community obligations.

CONCLUSION

When Sarita moved to Mexico City in the 1920s, she left behind her small native community with dirt roads, an irrigation system made of stone and dirt ditches, and one-story adobe houses surrounded by agricultural land. When she returned in the 1970s, Sarita lived in a very different and larger community with electricity, several schools, bus service, and running piped water. Yet, despite the changes, the egalitarian principles of water distribution remained consistent with earlier decades. La Purificación was still a place where residents enjoyed a greater measure of water security than other communities of the Valley of Mexico.

In La Purificación, as in numerous Mexican communities, water has long been the soul of the pueblo. Without water for drinking and growing food, people could not have settled this rocky foothill setting. The bulk of anthropological research on water control in Mexico has focused on the importance of irrigation systems for sustaining human populations. Indeed, when La Purificación was a small pueblo and every family relied on agriculture for subsistence and commercial activities, irrigation management defined community life. Now that families rely more on wage work, water for household use has taken on a more prominent place in community life, and the recently installed piped water system has affected the community's social organization.

The local history shows how the formation of La Purificación's modern piped water system draws on a traditional form of communal water management and, at the same time, incorporates new social and technological features. For hundreds of years, small communities in the northern Acolhuacan region have managed water as a collective resource, which depends on and strengthens social ties within each community. The Spanish Conquest and colonization shifted the flow of water to large-scale agriculture and elite social groups, a pattern that intensified after Mexican independence. The Mexican Revolution ushered in a new era of water politics that allowed smaller communities like La Purificación to regain control over precious water resources. Nevertheless, the federal government tended to place greater emphasis on developing agricultural resources such as irrigation rather than on improving rural drinking water systems. The major efforts during all of these periods focused on transporting surface water primarily for irrigation into the area where La Purificación is located. La Purificación has continuously struggled with other communities, haciendas, and various government entities to maintain its collective hold on water. As a result, individual water rights have always been subordinate to collective efforts. Gaining individual access to water has always meant abiding by local customary principles of communal resource distribution.

Since the 1970s, La Purificación has become incorporated into the industrial and urban culture of the Valley of Mexico. As a result, the importance of irrigation has declined and household water management has emerged as a primary concern for a broader segment of the population throughout northern Acolhuacan. The new water systems are not simply the result of the installation of outside technology, but rather form part of the long history of water control in this region of Mexico. The resulting shifts in the cargo system show how drinking water management has affected changes in the traditional set of civil and religious cargos. Most importantly, the historical legacy of communal resource management provided the foundation for a set of principles and values that persist, even as the distribution and uses for water changed. Even drinking water that runs through a modern system of pumps, pipes, and tanks retains its traditional value as the soul of the pueblo.

4/Leveling the Water
The Power of Civil and Religious *Cargos*

Effectively distributing water is more than simply an engineering feat; water distribution is also a social process. Certain individuals decide who should receive water, under what conditions, and at what cost. In La Purificación, the civil and religious *cargo* officers make these decisions by drawing on local cultural values, meanings, and practices.

Decision-making processes about proper water distribution often involve compromise and power struggles about who should control access to and use of local water sources. In the Valley of Mexico, as in other regions with limited water resources, individuals and groups with more power have more water. In other words, water is such an important resource in the Valley of Mexico's semi-arid environment that powerful groups use their influence to capture water for purposes that benefit their interests. Greater amounts of water are available to large-scale agricultural operations growing cash crops than are available for small-scale cultivators growing food crops for subsistence. And water flows more readily to large industry than to small firms, just as it is more available to Mexico City's wealthier neighborhoods than the poor ones. Unequal power relations can result in unequal access to water.

Yet, because water is so important to daily life and productive work, those who control water have a source of power over others who need the water. Out in the foothills of the Valley of Mexico, los Purifiqueños rely on their local political offices to prevent inequality from creeping into their community water system. Rather than particular individuals or corporations, the community maintains control over local water resources, and this community control of precious water resources allows local officials to control a range of important matters. One of the main goals of this community-based water system is to provide a level or *parejo* distribution of limited water resources so that all households can meet their basic water needs. In a region where many groups compete for scarce water supplies, how does La Purificación maintain its community control of water and ensure that water is distributed in an equitable manner? To address this question, I first focus on the structure of La Purificación's civil and religious cargos. In the next chapter, I explore how residents interact with cargo officials to obtain access to water.

PUMPS AND PIPES

The piped water system pumps groundwater electrically from a well and then channels it through large pipes to four stone holding tanks located at higher elevations. From there the water travels by gravity through smaller pipes and hoses to individual households. The community routinely rations the piped water to save on the costs of running the electric pump, and each section of the community receives at least two hours of water four days per week. In this way, households have nearly equal access to piped water.

Most households store water in rooftop water tanks as well as in plastic containers, metal drums, and plastic buckets. In addition, family compounds usually have a *pileta,* which is a rectangular concrete water reservoir used for doing laundry and washing dishes outdoors. Only about 20 percent of the houses have large, underground cisterns (*cisterna*) that hold 250 to 800 gallons of water. According to my estimates, an average household without a cistern typically has the capacity to store about 35 to 50 gallons of water per person per day in rooftop tanks and indoor and outdoor reservoirs. Without a public sewage system, most houses have septic tanks and also drain gray wastewater onto their properties, into irrigation canals, or into the streets.

Figure 4.1 Mayordomos *collect money from a resident. Similar to most houses, the one-story house has a rooftop tank for storing piped water.*

SEARCHING FOR EQUITY IN AN UNEVEN GEOGRAPHY

When authorities attempt to provide a level or *parejo* distribution of drinking water, they strive to ensure that each household receives a fair amount of drinking water. In other words, water distribution is not entirely even, especially due to the rugged mountainous topography. Obvious geographical differences make it difficult for authorities to provide equal amounts of water to each household, but they continuously seek ways to bring a sense of fairness to the distribution process.

One challenge to maintaining an equitable distribution system arises from the history of the infrastructure. Recall that the water well was installed in the *ejido,* which lies at a lower elevation west of the community nucleus. The largest pipes of the water system were initially installed in the western half of the community, called Barrio de Santa Teresa (see Figure 4.2). This barrio's northern section is at a higher elevation than the southern section. The large pipes drain water toward households at lower elevations. Although households at higher elevations in Barrio de Santa Teresa might receive water for about two hours every other day, households at the lower elevations receive up to six hours or more every other day.

By contrast, in the eastern half of the community—Barrio de La Concepción—households at high elevations of the north section barely receive two hours of water every other day, and some households at the highest elevations receive even less water. Households in the northern section of Barrio de La Concepción, which are farthest from the water pump and large water tanks, use metal and rubber pipes with smaller diameters that were installed years after the community initiated the piped drinking water project.

The *colonia,* the newest section of the community, experiences similar disparities. One section of households near a water tank receives water each day because the water passes through pipes that lead up to the main part of the community. The other section of the colonia rotates water delivery every other day between two groups of households.

Several factors have resulted in this unequal aspect of the water system. The installation of the drinking water system began in Barrio de Santa Teresa, the western half of the settlement and the section closest to the well. According to some previous water authorities, large water pipes were installed in the western barrio to deliver large quantities of groundwater for irrigation as well as domestic use. The earliest plans called for a reduction in the portion of surface water for the western barrio to replace the surface water with groundwater pumped up from the well. This plan was to allow the eastern half of the settlement, Barrio de La Concepción, to rely on a greater volume of surface water for irrigation and domestic purposes. Households in this barrio are closer to the incoming source of surface water, which enters the community through irrigation canals located at higher elevations in the eastern half of the community. Thus, the earliest projects installed the first two water tanks above the northern section of Barrio de Santa Teresa and large water pipes in both the northern and southern sections of the barrio, which resulted in draining large volumes of water to lower elevations. Authorities also said that efforts to install water meters have been difficult and costly, especially because the use of gravity to

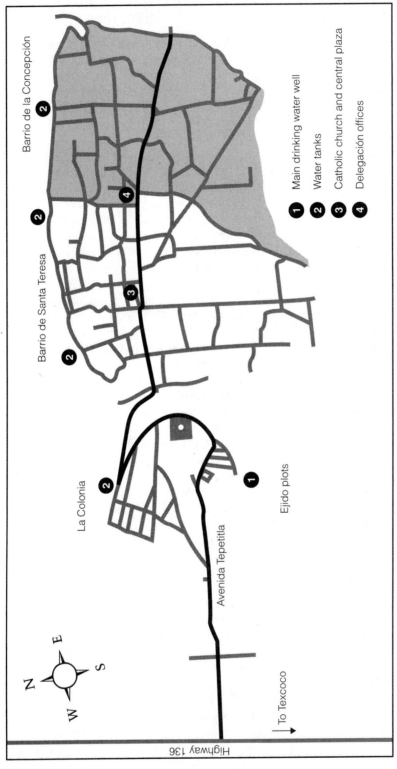

Figure 4.2 Map indicating La Purificación's barrios. Going from west to east, the barrio called La Colonia is at a lower elevation near the ejido plots. Barrio de Santa Teresa is the western half of the main part of the community and the location of the Catholic church and Delegación. Barrio de La Concepción is the eastern half of the community. Avenida Tepetitla is the main paved road and divides the community into north and south. The map shows the locations of the drinking water well and the four water tanks, which are all located on hillsides overlooking the barrios.

Barrio de la Concepción

Barrio de Santa Teresa

La Colonia

Avenida Tepetitla

Ejido plots

To Texcoco

Highway 136

① Main drinking water well
② Water tanks
③ Catholic church and central plaza
④ Delegación offices

channel water in the system creates more pressure than standard water meters can withstand.

As explained in the previous chapter, the community decided later to use groundwater for domestic use for the entire community and surface water solely for irrigation. But the infrastructure favored the western half of the community, making it difficult to channel water through an undeveloped infrastructure in the eastern barrio. Residents routinely complain about drinking water draining away from households located at higher elevations, particularly from Barrio de la Concepción, to lower elevations in Barrio de Santa Teresa. Despite this inequality, it was determined difficult and costly to replace water pipes and install valves to channel water to higher elevations. Authorities also said that once one part of the settlement began receiving adequate water supplies, it became more difficult to organize residents to work in *faenas* developing the drinking water system in the other areas of the community.

In some cases, household members claim that they do not receive a sufficient water supply and threaten not to pay their water fees. Authorities who make eyewitness inspections usually prove that sufficient water reaches these households—the water simply may not arrive in the quantity, the length of time, or the time of day that people in the household wish. Water authorities are long-term residents and have extensive knowledge about the flow of water within the community. They know what sections of the community receive sufficient quantities of water and what sections do not. Officials readily talk to friends and relatives in any part of the community to see if sufficient water reaches households located next to residents who claim to have problems with water delivery. This approach allows authorities to judge whether problems are confined to a particular household, for example due to a damaged pipe or connection, or if the problems involve pipes that supply several households. I observed many cases in which authorities decided that a person was making a false claim to get more than their fair share of water.

Carlos, president of the Drinking Water Committee, pointed out to me the advantages of having local residents manage the drinking water system. Local control of the water means the community controls costs and is better at responding to local residents. Established residents become aware of problems much faster than would be the case if they relied on the Municipio of Texcoco or another outside entity to manage their drinking water system. Carlos said that the community did not want the same problems—such as high costs, delayed projects, and nonresponsive government officials—that occur with road repair, school construction, and other projects highly dependent on outside support.

Local officials gain authority because of their knowledge of the water system and water delivery problems. The community elects people from each half of the settlement to serve on the Drinking Water Committee, which balances the knowledge of water distribution and water problems among residents. For example, authorities draw on their knowledge of the history of water development, the geography of water pipes and valves, the names of properties and their owners, customary ways of organizing faenas, and traditions of water control rooted in the history of irrigation management. They use their social knowledge to fairly distribute drinking water.

The 1994–1996 Drinking Water Committee included Carlos who lived in Barrio de Santa Teresa, and Pablo and Samuel, the committee's secretary and treasurer, respectively, who both lived in Barrio de la Concepción. So together they were familiar with each barrio's ongoing problems with drinking water delivery. Pablo, Samuel, and other residents from households with water problems occupied positions of authority to mobilize resources and deal with some of the problems. They knew, for example, when water had not reached their own households, so they could immediately assess whether the problem resulted from a broken pipe, the improper adjustment of a water valve, or failure to turn on the water pump at the required time to create enough pressure to carry water to the far eastern portion of the settlement. When other residents complained to Pablo about inadequate water delivery, he quickly pointed out that he too had not received water to bathe that morning and that he and the other officials were working on the problem to the best of their ability.

Committee members also regularly encounter neighbors from Barrio de La Concepción who complain about water problems; sometimes the officers joke with their neighbors that their names will be next on the roster for election to a cargo so they will have the opportunity to see how difficult it can be to address water problems. During my fieldwork, some of the residents in higher elevations in Barrio de La Concepción negotiated lower water fees and did not pay for some months when water did not reach their houses, but they were also obligated to provide leadership and labor to help improve water delivery to their households. These are examples of household members using their close ties to local power of the water authorities to make changes in how water is delivered to their households.

THE CARGO SYSTEM AND LEVELING

Because of the physical challenges of providing water in this mountainside setting, the community requires some mechanism for leveling out potential disparities. La Purifiación's cargo holders are the local authorities in charge of managing local water resources and handling other community manners. Each cargo is an unpaid but obligatory office to which people are elected that rotates among members of the community. Civil cargos last three years, and religious cargos last one year. The cargos are organized in a hierarchy of civil and religious offices. Civil–religious systems are well documented in anthropological studies of rural communities in Mexico and other Latin American countries (Stephen and Dow 1990). Cargo systems consist of a series of offices arranged in a hierarchy with a few offices at the top and many smaller offices at the bottom. Individuals, typically men, hold a lesser office before being selected for a higher office.

Cargo holders who occupy the highest offices tend to be elders of the community and have the most respect and prestige. Prestige refers to an individual's standing in the community. Residents with high prestige have higher standing and carry more influence in local affairs. Individuals gain prestige and status by volunteering their time and successfully completing their cargo service, which often involves giving time and resources to the community. As they successfully complete service in one cargo, they then move up the hierarchy to fulfill more prestigious cargos. In other words, an individual's prestige depends on giving things to the community rather than possessing and keeping wealth and resources. Some anthropologists have even reported on communities with waiting lists of individuals wanting to get the chance to hold a particular cargo (for example, see Cancian 1990, 1992).

Scholars debate the origin of cargo systems and whether the civil–religious hierarchies reflect deep indigenous roots or were responses to Spanish colonial pressures on community resources (for a review of the debates, see Stephen and Dow 1990). Part of these debates focus on whether cargo systems level out wealth differences (Tax 1937; Wolf 1955, 1957) or actually reinforce wealth differences (Cancian 1965). I agree that cargo systems may not equalize all wealth differences in a market economy, but they can potentially draw from noncapitalist practices and level some local aspects of social inequality. In this regard, I agree with anthropological perspectives of Mexican cargo systems that see them as dynamic and fluid institutions responding to historical and material social processes (Bonfil Batalla 1996; Roseberry 1989; Wolf 1986, 1990). Regardless of their origin, contemporary cargo systems can provide a measure of security for group members.

In my view, cargo systems are community institutions that have a leveling effect regardless of existing status differences. The leveling effect results from practices used to distribute local food, land, water, and other resources in egalitarian ways that provide a common benefit for group members. Leveling mechanisms are common among a wide variety of nonindustrial cultures in which members depend on each other for their livelihood. For example, Lee (2003) describes how the San hunter-gatherers of southern Africa share and distribute wild plants and animals as well as share use of limited water holes in the Kalahari Desert. The San use joking, kinship practices, naming traditions, and gift exchanges to promote and maintain egalitarian social relations that are essential in a sharing economy (Lee 2003, 59–123). Similarly, indigenous agricultural communities in the Andes of South America use religious fiestas to enhance egalitarian social relations and allow people to depend on each other for planting and harvesting crops as well as maintaining irrigation networks (Gelles 2000; Guillet 1992). Such leveling mechanisms maintain local economic practices that allow for an equitable distribution of vital water resources.

Below, I base the description of La Purificación's cargo system primarily on observations and interviews of particular cargo holders and participant observation of particular administrations of civil and religious authorities. Cargo systems are flexible institutions and vary across communities according to the structure and names of offices, the duties of cargo holders, and community priorities. Within communities, duties of each cargo vary and change according to each civil and religious administration. In my view, the flexible and dynamic character of cargo systems accounts for part of their success in addressing water issues and other important matters. Each year, La Purificación's civil and religious authorities discuss how to organize each group as well as how to coordinate relations between civil and religious cargos. People regularly bring new ideas into the system and try to organize activities in different ways each year.

Because gaining prestige in the community depends on successfully carrying out cargo service and engaging in activities that benefit the group, it is not surprising that some residents seek to outdo previous administrations and make their cargo service better, their work projects bigger, and their fiestas livelier.

WATER CONTROL AND CARGOS

Who are the individuals who strive to create a water system that is parejo? In La Purificación, direct day-to-day management of the piped water system is the responsibility of the Drinking Water Committee whose members hold cargos for three years. The committee's work, however, is embedded within the entire set of civil cargos of the municipal offices called the Delegación Municipal or simply the *delegación*. Civil cargo holders also coordinate their activities with religious cargo holders. This sort of civil–religious political organization has important consequences for drinking water management. Cargo officers of the Drinking Water Committee work with all local civil and religious authorities to create and enforce local policies that preserve the local drinking water supply as a communal resource. Only members of the community have the right to access the water supply as long as they abide by local traditions. Understanding the structure of La Purificación's cargo system is essential for understanding why the community does not regard water for household use as a commodity or a municipal service for which a household simply pays money.

Table 4.1 lists the names of each cargo and the number of officers in each cargo. La Purificación's cargo system incorporates principles described for

TABLE 4.1   CIVIL AND RELIGIOUS CARGO OFFICES

Civil Offices		**Number**
Delegación Municipal	Delegados	3
	Citizens' Participation Council	6
	Drinking Water Committee	18
	Irrigation Committee	6
	Social Patrol	40
	Auxiliary Committee of the Citizens' Participation Council for the Colonia	3
	Social Patrol for the Colonia	10
Ejido	Ejido Commissioners	6
	Security Council	6
Parents' Association	Kindergarten	6
	Elementary School	6
	Secondary School	6
Religious Offices		**Number**
Mayordomía del Pueblo	Fiscal or Fiscala	1 or 2
	Mayordomo or Mayordoma	19
Mayordomía del Culto	Fiscal or Fiscala	1 or 2
	Mayordomo or Mayordoma	19

nearby indigenous and nonindigenous *campesino* communities in the northern Acolhuacan region of the Valley of Mexico (Gómez Sahagún 1992; Palerm Viqueira 1993; Sokolovsky 1978, 1995). These obligatory offices require individuals to expend a great deal of their personal time, effort, and even personal resources. Most duties of civil cargos reflect national laws about municipal and ejido organization, but religious cargos and some civil cargos, including those dealing with water, follow local customary organization. A few cargos at the top of the hierarchy have the most responsibility and authority in the community, whereas a larger number of lower cargos have less responsibility and authority in local matters.

The civil cargos of the delegación and the ejido and the religious cargos of the *mayordomías* are obligatory and considered the most important authorities. Once called upon for one of these cargos, holders are expected to serve the term of the office or risk having community authorities impose sanctions on them. Sanctions can take the form of fines as well as withholding of water and other community services (see Chapter 5 for more details on sanctions). Other cargos, such as the education associations, are voluntary, and residents do not risk being penalized for declining to serve on those. All cargos require residents to coordinate their public service with their regular work. In most cases, the office holders maintain their regular work, but may adjust their work schedules to fulfill cargo duties. In most households, multiple family members help the elected office holder fulfill cargo duties, and some households pay non-household members to fulfill elected cargo officer's duties.

Community authorities coordinate activities among all the cargo offices, so each cargo holder consequently has the potential to make decisions that affect the management of the piped water system. Civil cargos rotate every three years among all households in the main part of the community. Religious cargos rotate every year among all households in the main part of the community. Residents living in a newly established barrio called a colonia are generally not included in these cargos. In general terms, men hold the civil cargos, but women were elected to the Drinking Water Committee for the first time in 2000. Established residents tend to hold the highest posts in each committee; they are also likely to have ties to agriculture by possessing both irrigation water and ejido land. All residents, including new residents, hold smaller cargos, which include bottom posts in the delegación, the social patrol, and education committees.

Residents use the word *faena* to refer to corvée labor, which involves obligatory unpaid community labor usually required of residents in lieu of or in addition to taxes for drinking water projects, road repair, and other public works projects. In numerous campesino communities throughout Mexico, it is common to find a system for mobilizing obligatory, unpaid communal labor to develop and maintain irrigation systems and other public works projects. Organizing and supervising communal labor is an important duty of most of La Purificación's civil and religious officers. The community's general faenas require that one representative of each household in the community be available for piped water projects and other projects that benefit all residents. Other faenas are required from only those households that directly benefit from a more specific project, such as projects related to irrigation, the ejido, and the schools.

TABLE 4.2   MAJOR ANNUAL FIESTAS SPONSORED BY RELIGIOUS OFFICERS

Date	Fiesta
January 6	Three Kings Day
January 24–February 1	Novena (nine days of rosaries and processions)
February 2–6	Virgin of the Candelaria
March (variable dates)	Palm Sunday, Holy Week, and Easter
June (variable dates)	Corpus Christi
July (variable dates)	Santo Jubileo
October 15	Santa Teresa
November 1–2	Day of the Dead Ceremonies
December 8	Virgin of the Immaculate Conception
December 12	Virgin of Guadalupe
December 24–25	Christmas and *Posadas*
December 31	New Year's Eve

TABLE 4.3   MAJOR ANNUAL FIESTAS SPONSORED BY CIVIL OFFICERS

Date	Fiesta	Main Sponsor
March (variable dates)	Carnival	Other Committee[a]
May 3	Holy Cross	Ejido
May 10	Mother's Day	Delegación and Parents' Associations
May 15	Fiesta of San Isidro	Ejido
July (variable dates)	School Graduations	Parents' Associations
September 14	Holy Cross	Other Committee
September 15	Independence Day	Delegación and Ejido
November 20	Revolution Day	Delegación and Ejido

[a]Other local groups sponsor fiestas that are not part of the obligatory duties of elected civil or religious cargo officials. Nevertheless, these fiestas typically involve coordination with civil and religious officials.

CIVIL CARGOS

Direct management of the piped water system is incorporated into the municipal offices called the Delegación Municipal, which is composed of a series of 33 cargos that each require three years of service. Three elected officials called *delegados* head the delegación and are considered the highest-ranking community officials. The delegados oversee three administrative committees: the Citizen's Participation Council, the Drinking Water Committee, and the Irrigation Committee. The delegados work closely with the presidents of the three committees to make decisions and manage civil affairs of the community. Delegados also oversee community service, which is work that each adult male between the ages of 18 and 60 is required to complete one day per month. Men are supposed to report to the delegados and request to fulfill some sort of work, such as cleaning a municipal building, working on public works projects, or completing other general tasks. The person may also pay 10 pesos each month instead of completing the service. Students are exempt from fulfilling this obligation. All of these civil authorities work closely with other community representatives to manage civil affairs in the community. Delegados supervise a social patrol (*guardia social*), a secretary, and a worker who cleans the office and performs other general office tasks.

The Citizens' Participation Council consists of a president, secretary, treasurer, and three auxiliary members. This committee oversees general public works projects, such as building and repairing roads, maintaining the cemetery, soliciting funds and materials for improving the schools and the medical clinic, and mobilizing residents to provide labor for public works.

The Drinking Water Committee consists of six top cargos: a president, vice-president, secretary, vice-secretary, treasurer, and vice-treasurer. The committee also has 12 auxiliary members called *fontaneros* who are in charge of operating the water pump as well as opening and closing valves in the piped water system. The committee oversees the day-to-day management of the piped water system for over 1,000 households with water connections.

The Irrigation Committee is in charge of managing the surface water used for irrigation (*agua de riego*). It consists of a president, secretary, and treasurer. Three auxiliary members called *aguadores* carry out the direct distribution of irrigation water to about 270 users. Members of the Irrigation Committee routinely work with authorities from other communities that share the surface water that flows from the sierra down to the foothills. As was mentioned in the previous chapter, the community used to rely on this source of water for irrigation and household purposes, so this committee was a precursor to the Drinking Water Committee.

The three delegados and the presidents of the three committees are the highest local authorities and occupy the most important cargos in the community. Within the Mexico's political system, the delegación is part of the Municipio of Texcoco. A *municipio* is comparable to a county in the United States. The Municipio of Texcoco is one of 125 municipios that make up the State of Mexico. The three delegados and the three top officers of the Citizen's Participation Council go to the Municipio of Texcoco at the beginning of their terms where they take their oath of office and receive identification badges and official municipio seals for stamping documents. These cargo holders have authority as representatives of the municipio and their signatures and seals are required for drinking water projects, including requests for construction materials and technical assistance from municipio, state, and federal programs.

The Drinking Water Committee directly oversees the day-to-day operation of the piped water system. Other officers, however, make decisions about water policy and often their signatures are required for matters related to the piped water system. On one hand, the Drinking Water Committee and the Irrigation Committee are subordinate to the delegados, who in turn are subordinate to municipio officials. On the other hand, the water committees exist outside of the municipio structure, which gives the community independence and autonomy from municipio control when it comes to water management. Community authorities strongly assert that this autonomy allows them to manage the water resources in ways that best meet the needs of local residents.

Community authorities do have ties to Mexico's broader political system and use these connections to obtain technical assistance and construction materials from the municipio and other government entities. Projects often require civil authorities to spend considerable time resolving water issues with other communities, municipio, state, and federal entities, legal officials, engineers, and suppliers of construction materials. Some of these discussions involve working with officials from national political parties. Like other areas of Mexico, members of Mexico's ruling Institutional Revolutionary Party or PRI (Partido Revolucionario Institucional) have tended to occupy the Municipio of Texcoco's political offices. Elected officials from the PRI and other PRI-organized programs were heavily involved in the earlier drinking water projects in La Purificación and surrounding communities. In the 1990s, political tensions emerged between the ruling PRI, which controlled the Municipio of Texcoco, and the new rival, the Party of the Democratic Revolution or PRD (Partido de la Revolución Democrática). The PRD won offices that controlled distribution of funds and materials for community development and, as a result, this rival party was taking credit for sponsoring drinking water projects in some communities. The projects of some communities were held up if they got caught in the regional political battles.

Guillermo, a civil official in La Purificación, said that, "if they want us to be PRI, we are PRI, and if they want us to be PRD, we are PRD," to obtain materials from the municipio for community drinking water projects. Carlos, the president of the Drinking Water Committee, commented that he thought the rivalry between political parties in the municipio sometimes benefits La Purificación by allowing authorities to play the rival parties against each other and obtain necessary materials and funds for public works. In fact, by having an autonomous cargo system without ties to national political parties, La Purificación has avoided political infighting with water resources, an issue that has occurred in other parts of Mexico (see Collier and Quaratiello 1999). La Purificación's nonpartisan approach to local government promotes more local cooperation, but partisan politics at higher levels of government can damage some drinking water efforts.

EJIDO CARGOS

The delegación also works with the 12 officers of the ejido. This ejido committee oversees matters for the 171 families with ejido land. Men usually occupy the offices, but some women have served as officers. During their three-year position, officers are exempt from being elected to other civil and religious offices. Ejido officers meet once a week to coordinate their own faenas and to organize ejido projects and meetings of all of the ejido families. Ejido cargos are civil cargos that stand outside of the delegación. According to some officers, an ejido cargo is not as burdensome as civil cargos in the delegación because the ejido manages little infrastructure and little agricultural equipment. The water well and pump are located in the ejido, so the ejido officials are involved in community water policy. In fact, the highest ranking delegación cargo holders invariably include at least one *ejidatario*. Because the ejido authorities are part of a federal system of ejidos, they also regularly interact with federal authorities and other national organizations.

RELIGIOUS CARGOS

Religious cargo holders are also community officials. Each year, 40 residents from separate households are elected to fulfill one year of obligatory religious cargo service to organize and sponsor annual festivals for the local Roman Catholic church. The group is divided into two mayordomía groups with about 20 members each. The men are called *mayordomos* and the women are called *mayordomas*. One or two members head each mayordomía group. A male leader is called the *fiscal* and a female leader is called the *fiscala*. The leaders keep account of the money collected to sponsor fiestas and coordinate work and monetary obligations of the mayordomos and mayordomas.

Residents of all socioeconomic strata are elected to serve in the mayordomías, which requires regular labor obligations such as cleaning the church property each week, preparing the church for fiestas, and going door-to-door to collect fiesta contributions from all the households in the community. Holding a religious cargo also involves giving monetary contributions to pay for food, music, and decorations for religious festivals. Wealthier people with extensive land and water holdings and other forms of wealth are often assigned the equivalent of two mayordomías, which obligates them to make larger contributions for the festival expenses. The mayordomos and mayordomas have regular meetings to discuss the amount of money and the kind of work each person will contribute to organizing the annual fiestas.

La Purificación has two mayordomía groups. One group, the Mayordomía del Pueblo, organizes the community's largest fiesta for its patron saint, the Virgin of the Candelaria whose feast day is February 2 (the feast day is called Candelmas Day in English and celebrates the purification of the Virgin Mary and the presentation of the baby Jesus in the temple 40 days after his birth). The Mayordomía del Pueblo also organizes activities for other religious holidays during the first half of the year, including Palm Sunday, Holy Week and Easter, and a smaller fiesta for Santa Teresa, the patron saint of the chapel in the western half of the community. The other group, the Mayordomía del Culto, organizes activities for the second half of the year, including the community's second largest fiesta for Corpus Christi, which takes place in June. The fiesta is celebrated on a Thursday, but, like Easter, the exact date varies according to the church calendar. The group also organizes a smaller fiesta for Santo Jubileo and for the Virgin of the Concepción, the patron saint of the small chapel of the eastern half of the community. The two groups carry out some of their activities independently of each other, but the two groups usually work together for the major fiestas. They also work together for Christmas festivities, the Fiesta of the Cross in September, the celebration of the priest's birthday, and other smaller religious activities.

Unlike civil cargos, which have direct ties to outside political officials, the religious cargos have few ties to outside religious officials. In other words, the mayordomías are part of La Purificación's parish and not part of the official Catholic church structure. As far as I am aware, every foothill and sierra community in northern Acolhuacan has similar religious cargo systems. The mayordomías organize their elections and carry out most duties independent of the

Figure 4.3 Residents participate in the annual Corpus Christi fiesta. To the left is a small sign that advises people to contact local authorities before purchasing property to see if piped water and sewage connections are included.

local priest, the bishop, or other religious officials of the Texcoco diocese. The religious cargo holders work with the local priest to organize the priest's duties such as officiating at masses during festivals. They also maintain church property, which includes the priest's apartment, office, and garage for parking his car. Religious officers also pay someone to clean the church buildings daily, ring the bell for religious activities, and assist the priest during each mass.

The autonomy of the religious cargos is expressed in a ceremony for installing the new mayordomos and mayordomas at the beginning of January. This ceremony takes place during a mass in which the outgoing mayordomos and mayordomas welcome the incoming office holders. Likewise, the outgoing fiscales turn over ceremonial staffs and the keys to church property to the incoming fiscales. The fiscales are responsible for the church property and possessions and keep close watch over the seventeenth-century church, which includes valuable antique objects such as gold chalices, embroidered cloths, and religious paintings and statues. The fiscales also watch over supplies such as candles, incense, altar cloths, and crosses.

Most importantly, the religious cargo holders have the authority to open and close the church for religious ceremonies, including life-cycle rituals. For example, when a couple plans a wedding, they contact the priest to select a day and time for the ceremony. The couple, however, must receive permission from the fiscales to use the church for the wedding ceremony. Without such permission, the couple cannot use the church for their event. Numerous times the fiscales have refused to open the church for a wedding or funeral for families who had not been paying their fiesta contributions or who had refused to complete religious cargo duties.

I talked about these practices to my friend Adolfo when he was a fiscal.

I asked, "The priest doesn't have keys to open the church?"

"That's right," he said.

I asked, "Have you ever not opened the church for a wedding?"

Adolfo smiled and said, "Of course!"

He recounted the case of the Vázquez family who wanted to have a wedding in the church. The Vázquez family, however, had not been contributing the annual fees to support the fiestas, and they had turned down the invitation to hold a religious cargo when it was their turn to serve. Adolfo notified the family that if they wanted permission to use the church, then they would have to pay their fiesta debts and agree to hold a religious cargo the next year. The Vázquez family complained to the priest and the civil authorities, but in the end they paid their fiesta debts and agreed to hold a religious cargo the following year. Adolfo drew up a letter outlining the agreement and gave a copy of the letter to the civil authorities so that the family would abide by the agreement.

I asked, "So did that take care of the problem?"

He responded, again with a smile, "Not quite."

He explained that the mayordomía groups pay for the flowers themselves and adorn the church each week. He explained that it is customary for the family sponsoring a wedding to pay for a dozen bouquets of flowers to adorn the altars and side niches of the church. Families usually like to select flowers that match the dresses and flowers of the bride and other members of the wedding party. The Vázquez family, however, refused to provide flowers to decorate the church. The day of the wedding, Adolfo removed all the flowers from the church so that the ceremony took place without the usual adornments.

"This was sad," he said. "But that is the way we do things. If they don't like it, they can find another church for their ceremonies."

This story illustrates the autonomy of the religious cargo holders to make decisions about such religious activities. This sort of case also reflects a broader leveling practice in La Purificación. Residents expecting to benefit from community resources, such as in this case the use of the church for a life-cycle ceremony, must fulfill customary community obligations. The local authorities have the right to refuse church access to families who do not make customary contributions to the church. The priest has little say in these matters. From the point of view of Adolfo, it would not be fair to allow any people to use the beautiful old church if they had not also made contributions to help preserve and maintain the property. In the next chapter, I illustrate ways that this same customary principle extends into cases regarding access to community water supplies and the cemetery.

This case of the Vázquez wedding also shows how mayordomos and mayordomas coordinate some activities with delegación cargo holders. Most importantly, civil and religious officials meet and develop ways for dealing with residents who do not want to accept a religious cargo. The meetings might result in a written agreement about how much to charge a person who is willing to pay money instead of doing the work of a mayordomo. In other words, some people try to pay their way out of completing the tasks required of being an office holder for a year. Civil and religious officials might also develop strategies to impose sanctions on people who do not accept mayordomías and others who do not fulfill their religious service. In addition to dealing with customary cargo obligations, religious officers routinely work with delegación officers to plan fiesta activities. The delegación, for instance, ensures that the local social patrol will watch over religious processions and dances in the plaza during fiestas. Civil authorities also give festival organizers permission to hold certain events on community property.

OTHER CARGOS

In addition to the major civil and religious cargos, the community has a series of other nonobligatory cargos. Such cargos include the educational committees for the kindergarten, the six-year primary school, and the three-year secondary school. Each school has a Parents' Association. All parents of children attending a school belong to the school's association, and the association elects officers. Women usually hold most of these cargos. These officers are elected for one year and, unlike other cargos, are not exempt from serving in the civil cargos and the mayordomías. Those with a heavier cargo in the delegación, church, or ejido would decline to be named to a cargo in the school, but some people with cargos in the school have to accept and serve in obligatory cargos when elected, although they usually leave the school cargo to carry out the heavier duties of obligatory cargo office. Education associations organize fiestas and faenas, coordinate policy with the directors and teachers, and charge fees for parents. They also coordinate activities with local civil officials and petition for government funds to improve school facilities.

Residents also participate each year in other forms of community service that people call cargos. Some of this service consists of participation in the following groups: a marching band for annual religious processions and patriotic parades; a folkloric dance group for patriotic ceremonies; a committee responsible for decorating the main portal for the two major religious fiestas; and a committee for organizing Independence Day festivities. Other forms of community service also do not count as fulfilling obligatory community service. In the church, for example, the mayordomía officials invite people to sponsor rosaries during the months of May and June and to sponsor parts of the Christmas celebrations. The church also has a number of voluntary associations that sponsor masses and small feast days for particular saints. In terms of civil activities, residents also participate in government-sponsored development programs, such as a milk distribution program for lower income families with young children. When working on such local projects, residents refer to their positions as cargos. Fulfillment of the duties of these cargos is voluntary and carries the same authority or responsibility of the major civil and religious cargos.

Nevertheless, participation in any cargo reinforces the notion that one is a full member of the community. Such practices relate to the broader cultural pattern of leveling out the work associated with developing a community support structure. One becomes a member of the community by contributing to the community, and all community work, whether marching in a band or working with a government-sponsored program, takes the form of some sort of cargo.

CARGO ELECTIONS

The changes in cargo elections particularly illustrate the close connection between water and local political organization. I had become curious about the cargo election process since beginning my fieldwork. When I met Adolfo in 1993, I was surprised to find a single man in his late twenties heading the may-ordomía. The ethnographic studies of indigenous communities in Chiapas and Oaxaca had reported that married men hold religious cargos and older men tend to hold the highest posts (for example, see Cancian 1992). La Purificación had also begun electing women to religious posts in the 1980s, something that I had found reported for very few other areas, although women are involved in communities that elect male–female couples to mayordomías (Mathews 1985; Stephen 1991). When I asked Adolfo how they select residents for La Purificación's religious cargos, he said the election process is parejo, meaning that elections are carried out in an even or level manner. All residents are eligible and obligated to hold the cargos when they are called upon.

Later, during my fieldwork of 1995–1996, I shifted my research focus to water management and the election of civil cargos. Manuel was the secretary of the Irrigation Committee and he was particularly helpful in explaining the intricacies of the election process. I had good rapport with Manuel because I had been talking with him informally for several months while I observed the daily operations of the Irrigation and Drinking Water committees. Like his cousin Adolfo, Manuel was single and in his twenties, and I asked him how it was that he came to occupy such a high post in the civil cargos. I told him that I assumed older married men would take up such work.

Manuel first explained to me that electing residents to cargos changed after the community installed the piped water system in the late 1970s. Before that time, cargo holders had to be men with rights to irrigation water and most, if not all, were married. Those with more water rights were selected more often and for some of the top posts. In the 1980s, the community instituted a new rotation schedule that included every household and not just those with irrigation water. This arrangement seemed fairer because more people were migrating into the community and they were not involved in the irrigation system. Yet, everyone was becoming hooked up to the newly installed drinking water system. As a result, cargos were rotated among all the households with drinking water.

Manuel explained how the rotation of cargos works. Every year, 40 residents are elected to serve in the mayordomías. They are selected from each half of the community and roughly correspond to a couple of blocks of houses along one or two streets. Approximately 20 office holders represent a group of adjoining households located in the western half of the community and the other 20 office holders come from a group of adjoining households in the eastern half of the community. The following year, the elections rotate to other adjoining houses. At the end of their term, office holders meet to discuss who among their neighbors with adjoining properties ought to be elected for the following year. They

Figure 4.4 Manuel (seated left) explains the process for electing civil and religious cargo *officers.*

bring their recommendations to a community assembly to be voted on by household representatives. In this way, the roster of eligible office holders rotates from section to section in the two halves of the community. The election rotates from one part of the community to the next, so that if a resident has a neighbor in the mayordomía, a resident can expect to be elected to office within the next one or two years.

Manuel explained that the same system is used for the civil cargos, but residents occupy these offices for three years. There are roughly 33 civil posts to fill, and residents never occupy a civil and religious post at the same time. Thus, during any year, nearly 90 household members hold the major cargos in the delegación, ejido, and mayordomías. Residents regularly talk about the number of years it will take for their household to become eligible for either civil or religious cargos. They often joke with their neighbors that they are next up on the list.

Like other residents, Manuel described the rotation system for cargo elections as parejo because every family or property owner is obligated to provide community service in an office when called upon. The use of the term *parejo* is interesting because it relates to the concept of a leveling mechanism that anthropologists use to talk about cargo systems. In La Purificación, residents distribute the cargos in an egalitarian way so that everyone shares the burden of community service. This acts to redistribute sources in the community because cargo holders contribute their own food, money, and labor for other residents. Religious cargo holders, for instance, meet their obligations by spending a substantial portion of their own money to sponsor fiestas. This is a leveling process because a portion of each cargo officer's resources is redistributed to the group rather than accumulated by individuals. In turn, the community distributes community resources so that everyone benefits in a similar manner.

I should stress, however, that this leveling mechanism does not redistribute all resources and does not put everyone on the same social and economic status. Obvious wealth differences persist and intensify as the region's former campesino economy transforms into a stratified, industrial, wage economy. In other words, the cargo system is not leveling out wealth differences but simply redistributing labor, food, water, and other resources. Among established residents, some families have more land and irrigation water and are involved as merchants selling flowers and medicinal herbs in city markets. Other families have no land and work for low wages locally or in nearby cities. Some new residents work as lawyers, engineers, and professors, and other newcomers live in small homes and work for meager wages as day laborers, domestic workers, and seamsters doing piecework for clothing manufacturers. These wealth differences remain in place and have steadily increased as the region becomes more enmeshed in the Valley of Mexico's industrial, capitalist economy.

Although not leveling wealth differences, La Purificación's cargo system does even out the access to water as well as the burdens associated with community-based water management. The rotating schedule for electing cargo holders helps to ensure that wealthy households do not have all the water whereas the poor households are left with little water to meet daily needs, which occurs far too often in urban areas of the Valley of Mexico. Furthermore, the cargo system does not unfairly burden poorer families by asking them to provide all the labor to community projects. Even if socioeconomic inequalities exist, Manuel is correct when he says that the community's cargo system is parejo because it has an egalitarian management approach.

Despite the egalitarian character of the cargo system, I did notice that the highest cargos reveal nonegalitarian tendencies in the election process. I asked Manuel why native-born male residents who have ties to local agriculture and use irrigation water tend to occupy the higher civil cargos. I noticed the same tendency for the highest religious cargos. Manuel said that this aspect of the election process was necessary because new residents have different approaches to community issues. He said new residents often view water as a commodity and a private service for which they simply pay money, so even if they are wealthy and have more formal education, they are not elected to the powerful cargo positions charged with maintaining a communal management approach. Thus, the process of electing people to civil and religious cargos concentrates power in the hands of established residents, and the established residents have a greater interest in and experience with managing water as a communal resource.

Cargo elections represent a paradox: Everyone is equally eligible to be elected to a cargo. But to ensure that everyone gains equal access to water and other community resources, the election process is unequal in that it allows only individuals to hold office if they are likely to enforce local egalitarian principles. I asked Manuel how the community carried out this form of election process. The rotation schedule, he said, is supposed to move in an orderly fashion among all households and select a balance of individuals from each half of the community. Nevertheless, to choose suitable candidates for top civil cargos, authorities may propose someone whose name is not on the rotation schedule. Manuel referred to this method of selecting top officers as "skipping and hopping" about the community. He explained that the highest offices require people who have lived in the community for many years; they must know the local customs and must have participated in other forms of community service before having a top cargo.

Manuel used himself as an example. Although he was relatively young for a top irrigation cargo, he had represented his father's household in a prior mayordomía. Furthermore, he and his brothers had worked as aguadores, which are irrigation cargo holders who directly distribute the irrigation water to each property. As a native-born Purifiqueño, Manuel knew the customs and had extensive kinship ties in the community. When the rotation of civil cargos included his name on the list of eligible candidates, he seemed like a good choice for the irrigation cargo. Compared to other residents, especially new residents with little or no connection to the irrigation system, Manuel had the knowledge and skills needed to fulfill the cargo duties.

Manuel also explained that the delegados and presidents of each civil committee in particular must know community customs, as well as be able to work hard and organize others to work together. He noted that some residents are selected for some of the top posts if they are able to rearrange their work schedule to be present in the delegación, and that it is advantageous to elect top officers who have vehicles and phones to be able to carry out their duties.

At the same time that delegación officers discuss whom to elect, the residents with ejido land discuss whom to elect to serve ejido cargos for the same three-year period. The elections of new officers for ejido cargos are purposefully held a few months before the election of delegación officers. According to Manuel, while the ejidatarios select residents to occupy ejido cargos, they also reserve a few candidates to fill civil posts in the delegación. In particular, the ejidatarios attempt to reserve at least one resident with ejido land who could be elected as one of the three top posts as a delegado. In this way, Manuel explained, the interests of the ejido are represented in each administration of civil authorities. Because only established families possess ejido lands, this principle guarantees that families with local knowledge of communal water traditions control the water system.

Manuel's explanations fit with other explanations I later elicited from other cargo holders, and his views fit with my observations once I traced elections back a few decades and identified who had been a cargo holder and whether they were established residents or newcomers. I concluded that La Purificación's election process limits some residents from gaining access to more powerful posts in the cargo system. In particular, new residents without ties to agriculture are less likely to be elected as delegados or heads of committees in the delegación. During the election process, civil officials first identify those qualified to fill these top civil cargos and then use the list of eligible households to elect residents to lesser cargos. Professionals and people who may be highly educated and have high incomes are elected to bottom cargos and are rarely elected to the highest cargos. New residents, regardless of their wealth and education, have not been elected to top cargos. Like Manuel, all the cargo holders I interviewed justified this election process by saying that new residents are not familiar with the customary rights and obligations. As a result, new residents, women, and residents who engage in wage labor with little or no ties to local agriculture tend to occupy lower cargos and fulfill small, short-term tasks such as being a group leader to notify other residents about faenas.

Moreover, the civil and religious rotation schedules exclude residents living in the newer colonia, as most of these individuals are new residents to La Purificación. Although these new residents will never occupy the most powerful offices, the civil authorities can use their discretion to elect colonia residents to mayordomías, but not to lead a mayordomía; officials may also elect colonia residents to lower-ranking civil cargos, but not as delegados, or heads of the Drinking Water Committee or other major committees. The population of the colonia consists overwhelmingly of new residents of lower socioeconomic households. The community elects a few colonia residents as auxiliary members of the Citizen's Participation Council and expects all colonia residents to fulfill specific types of annual community labor obligations such as sponsoring part of the Christmas fiestas and cleaning the cemetery grounds before Day of the Dead ceremonies that start on November 1. Colonia residents are not elected to the Drinking Water Committee and have very little representation in other civil offices that influence water management. Because irrigation water is not channeled to the colonia, colonia residents do not serve on the Irrigation Committee. In the 1970s, the earliest settlers of the colonia signed land contracts that stated that they would be exempt from fulfilling cargo service but that they would be obligated to fulfill other community positions regarding civil and religious matters. Many colonia residents complain about having to submit to the community's authority without being able to occupy the higher positions of authority.

HOW IS THIS LEVELING?

The ethnographic details in this chapter illustrate how the community uses its local civil–religious hierarchy of offices to maintain power and thus be able to control water resources. We might summarize this process by saying that those with local political power control water, and those with water maintain local political power. In other words, the hold on water gives water managers a source of power, which they use to maintain an even water system that places a high value on an egalitarian approach to distributing drinking water to the residents of La Purificación. This leveling of the water, in turn, relates to the contention that drinking water rights and obligations are supposed to be *parejo*—a term with multiple meanings related to notions of being level, even, fair, and just. Water is a vital but difficult resource to secure on an individual basis in the Valley of Mexico's rugged geography and contentious social setting. The history of water control in the region indicates competing ways of distributing water for household consumption, and many of the predominant approaches in urban areas of the valley favor wealthier citizens and corporations. Not so in La Purificación.

La Purificación's leveling process occurs because the positions of authority are rotated among many members of the community. From a comparative view, La Purificación's system is different than political systems in other societies where leaders are chosen based on heredity or from elite social classes.

Residents tolerate inequalities in water distribution if the inequalities are due to geographical and technical factors and not the result of a few residents purposefully benefiting at the expense of others. Residents put up with the natural and technical disparities, but los Purifiqueños work hard to identify and address social inequities that bring about unnecessary forms of water-related suffering. With its local power and local egalitarian principles, La Purificación provides its residents with sufficient water needed to provide a relatively healthy and comfortable life in the foothills. For many residents, the benefits of accessing precious water resources outweigh the burdens of community participation.

5/"It's Our Custom"
Water Rights and Obligations

Local civil officials oversee the process by which any household connects to La Purificación's piped water system. A household must do more than simply request a water hook up (*toma* in Spanish) from local authorities and pay water fees. The community grants water access to residents who follow customary law and fulfill customary obligations. In addition to paying water fees, other civil and religious obligations include providing monetary contributions and engaging in community service activities that may or may not directly relate to water management. Residents sign water contracts stating that they understand and agree to fulfill both civil and religious obligations.

Los Purifiqueños regard groundwater as a locally controlled communal resource that community members share and manage in common.[1] In other words, groundwater is not private property owned by an individual, nor is it a commodity sold by a government agency or private business. Because groundwater for domestic use is a communal resource, residents gain a right to the water by fulfilling obligations associated with community membership. Water rights and obligations are embedded within a dynamic and flexible set of general customary laws that residents refer to as *usos y costumbres*. When I asked why they manage water this way, residents often said "It is our custom," or "That's the way things are here." As a body of customary law, most water rights are unwritten and passed on orally, whereas some are developed at community assemblies and written as resolutions. Most customary laws revolve around water as the community's most important resource shared in common.

As noted in the previous chapter, residents elected to the highest civil *cargos* in the *delegación* tend to come from established families who have an interest in managing piped water as a communal resource. The election of local officials reflects general support for the local system of water management. At times, however, officials must deal with residents who oppose aspects of the prevailing

[1] I use the term *communal* in a general sense to refer to a resource held in common by a group. The term does not refer to Mexico's more restrictive designation of a federally recognized agricultural collective or cooperative ejido.

form of water management. In particular, new residents who move from urban areas to La Purificación tend to view household water as a commodity and think that water service ought to be provided based solely on one's ability to pay. Some wealthier residents claim that households ought to be able to consume as much water as they can afford rather than gaining access by sponsoring religious fiestas and fulfilling other customary nonmonetary obligations.

This outside view ignores local customs that place water rights within a broader local cultural heritage. Every household has access to a minimum amount of water, and paying more money or fulfilling more obligations does not allow individuals to get more water than other residents. All civil authorities in the delegación, not simply the authorities of the Drinking Water Committee, control some aspect of the piped water system. This shared control of the community's most precious resource allows authorities to band together to counter pressures to manage water as a commodity and distribute it in an unequal fashion.

REQUESTING ACCESS TO WATER

La Purificación authorities draw on local practices of water management, which include cutting off water to any household that refuses to fulfill their community obligations. In the introduction to this book, I explained how I first discovered that authorities cut off drinking water when residents failed to sponsor religious fiestas. Such practices show that there is no explicit relationship between the right to piped water and any particular custom. For as long as any resident can remember, the community has followed rules similar to those used for managing the irrigation system, which relies on a surface water source. The recent development of a system for piping groundwater to households has incorporated the same principle of cutting off piped water for not fulfilling community obligations. When the piped water system was first being installed in the late 1970s, each household seeking access provided monetary contributions. In addition, residents participated in *faenas*—unpaid labor—to dig wells, install pumps, lay large pipes over the mountainous terrain, build large water tanks, and install the network of pipes in each section of the community. Thus, los Purifiqueños view the water system as a product of a longer community history of working together for a common benefit. Since the initiation of the piped water project, residents have associated the right to piped water with historically rooted practices of fulfilling community civil and religious obligations.

By the 1980s, the installation of a piped water system and other infrastructure brought about social changes. Most important, perhaps, is the fact that piped water makes it easier for people to live independently of irrigation water and make a living by commuting to wage jobs outside of the community. When new immigrants settle in the community, they expect to obtain piped water as a paid service, much as they did when living in urban areas. In addition, a younger generation of established residents has built their own houses and is requesting piped water service without having engaged in the work to install the system. The existence of new types of households has prompted authorities to develop new water policies and practices, but these new water practices remain consistent with traditional water values and practices.

Figure 5.1 Requesting a household water connection from drinking water authorities. In this picture, the young man (right) shows the president of the Drinking Water Committee paperwork indicating that he has fulfilled his community obligations, including recently serving as a religious cargo *officer.*

Changes in water management have changed the process by which individuals become recognized as community citizens with rights to access community resources. Decades prior in La Purificación and other nearby *campesino* communities, one became a community resident through birth or marriage, and outsiders were restricted from purchasing land or gaining rights to irrigation water. Now more land is being sold to outsiders. Residents in the La Purificación recall that customary laws about land ownership lasted until the late 1960s when it became difficult to make a living by agriculture and land became more valuable to sell to outsiders in small plots for residential use. Selling land has become a private transaction involving an exchange of money between buyer and seller. After purchasing land, new owners are supposed to meet with delegación authorities and register land transactions, but many delay this process. Years may pass between the time someone purchases a property and begins constructing a new home. In such cases, those who purchase land delay officially registering as community residents.

When starting to build houses, new residents invariably first contact civil authorities to register and request piped water service. New residents can purchase land and construction material and request electric service on their own, but requesting piped water for the household requires meeting with civil cargo holders. At that meeting, new residents discover that they cannot pay for water in the same way they paid for their land and electric service. Civil cargo officers explain to new residents that the cost of obtaining the right to access the community water supply entails the fulfillment of customary obligations in addition to paying water fees. New residents with family ties to the community understand and accept this requirement. Newcomers without previous ties to the community are less likely to understand the local customs and often express dismay to learn that obtaining piped water is linked to such duties as sponsoring fiestas and completing faenas. With no other alternative piped water supply, newcomers eventually accept the customs and obtain access to the precious liquid.

CATEGORIES OF WATER CONSUMPTION

One Saturday afternoon, Juan arrived at the desk of the Drinking Water Committee to talk to Carlos, the committee president, about obtaining a drinking water connection. Juan, a quiet and serious young man in his twenties, wore jeans and a dark leather jacket. Juan lived with his parents, but he recently married and had a young baby. He was planning to build his own house on his family's property. Carlos explained that the community charges for a water connection, and Juan said he knew it was a lot of money, but as a son of a longtime resident, he expected to pay less than other people. "And I was in the *mayordomía* last year," said Juan. He showed Carlos a slip of paper indicating that he had completed his religious cargo service. Carlos and Juan eventually settled on the fee of 2,000 pesos for the water connection.

When I was observing at the Drinking Water Committee desk on another Saturday afternoon, María spoke to Carlos about obtaining a drinking water connection. María was friendly and readily laughed while talking with Carlos. She wore a short skirt, high-heeled shoes, and a lot of makeup and jewelry, which was unusual for women of the rural community but characteristic of newcomers moving from urban areas. María explained how glad she was to finally leave Mexico City and settle in a more peaceful and quiet country setting. She and her husband planned to start building their house now that they bought a local property. Carlos described some of the water issues facing La Purificación and noted that purchasing property did not automatically guarantee a water connection. "But I need water," said María. Carlos told her that the fee would be about 8,000 pesos. María was visibly shocked. I too was surprised when I heard the amount Carlos planned to charge María, an amount that I knew was nearly four times more than the amount charged Juan. Carlos and María discussed the issue further and when she came back the next week, they settled on a fee of about 6,000 pesos. Why, I wondered, did drinking water authorities charge different fees for water connections? To me, this unequal treatment seemed to go against the egalitarian principles I had been documenting.

Carlos and other authorities explained why the community takes such approaches when residents ask for water connections. Established residents claim a right to piped water because they contributed money and labor during the initial installation of the piped water system. To established residents, it is unjust that new residents like María, who were not involved in the initial development of the piped water system, nonetheless expect to have piped water access without making similar labor contributions. As Fidel, the head of the Citizen's Participation Council, once told me, newcomers like María "want to come to eat dinner without having helped set the table." The outsider attitude just seemed downright unfair to Fidel and most other long-time residents.

Consequently, the community has developed policies for charging households for the right to piped water and for registering new household water connections. These emergent policies constantly change with each new administration of civil authorities and with discussions at annual community assemblies. In 1995, for example, authorities instituted a new fee structure for household connections to the water system based on three categories that corresponded to one's residential status in the community. First, officials charged 2,000 pesos or less to native residents who had contributed to the initial development and management of the water system and who had fulfilled other community obligations. Second, officials charged a middle category of between 2,000 and 4,000 pesos to residents of a younger generation who come from established families, such as Juan. They may not have contributed to earlier water projects, but they have fulfilled cargo service and made other contributions to the community. Third, officials charged the highest fees of between 6,000 and 8,000 pesos to nonnatives and even some established residents who had never contributed to community projects. In other words, new residents provided two or three times more money than established residents to obtain the right to piped water and register a household water connection.

These water connection categories partly illustrate the relationship between residency status and socioeconomic stratification. Many established residents view new residents as wealthier than campesino families, particularly if new residents are professionals or merchants who purchase large properties for residential use and drive expensive automobiles and trucks. Established residents with ties to agriculture view themselves as lower-income campesinos and expect to be able to receive a right to piped water in exchange for fulfilling labor obligations rather than solely in exchange for money. Many households in the *colonia* consist of new residents of the lower socioeconomic status, but they arrived before these categories were established and avoided paying the higher access fees.

These categories pertain to obtaining a household connection to the piped water system, and all residents register the water for noncommercial household use with the Drinking Water Committee. Each registered user is authorized to have a connection that is no larger than a pipe with a half-inch diameter, a requirement that is part of Mexico's national water policies. To date, no categories for commercial use of the piped water have been established and the community has prohibited the use of connections larger than the standard-sized pipe. Ongoing discussions and disputes have ensued about how to charge water fees for new commercial uses, such as restaurants, hair salons, dry-cleaning and laundry services, and greenhouses. Established residents control the piped water system and have not instituted higher commercial fees for water, especially because established residents are more likely than new residents to use piped water for local commercial activities. Community assemblies have passed resolutions to charge greenhouse users for piped water consumption, but there is no indication that this has ever been enforced. Generally, greenhouse owners are established residents who obtained water connections when the system was originally installed for both irrigation and household use. In a few cases, greenhouse owners paid for a household water connection at the rate of the lowest category and used the water to supplement irrigation water supplies. Water authorities told me that this has become increasingly difficult for others to do once community residents voted at assemblies to reserve groundwater for household purposes.

Residents request the right to piped water by negotiating with all delegación authorities and not simply with members of the Drinking Water Committee. When community residents go to the Drinking Water Committee to request a water connection, they are usually surprised that the fee is at least 6,000 pesos. Residents making such requests usually ask if it is possible to get a lower rate and, like Juan, offer proof that they have contributed money and labor to earlier water projects and other civil and religious activities. Some show receipts for contributions to water projects and official receipts of completed labor obligations. The Drinking Water Committee also requires the resident to fill out a form that must include signatures and seals of the *delegados,* the Citizen's Participation Council, and the Irrigation Committee. The signatures confirm that the residents are up to date on their payments and have fulfilled community service obligations for social patrol duty and faenas. If they are not up to date in any of these payments, they must pay their debts before receiving required signatures. In some cases, residents prove that they have completed a year of religious mayordomía service, which allows them to be exempt from a year of other types of community fees and service obligations. In many cases, residents have to discharge previous unpaid obligations by paying money or contributing bags of cement equivalent to the number of missed faenas. Civil authorities sometimes charge a higher category of 8,000 pesos to residents who refuse to be up to date in their payments. The Drinking Water Committee distributes the money among the other civil committees to cover the residents' debts.

Most authorities recognize that they are charging a large amount of money for the right to piped water and for establishing a registered household water connection. Authorities explain that the money is used to help pay for improvements and repairs of the system as well as day-to-day costs such as paying electric bills for the water pumps. Authorities justify the higher categories for new residents by pointing out that the water system is expensive to run and that the community needs to recover costs from new users who benefit from the system but who did not contribute money or labor during the initial development of the system. In some ways, the water connection fee is like paying for a share in the communal water system. Authorities also indicate that new residents are less likely in the future to contribute labor or money to drinking water projects, so that, in their view, it is necessary to apply such charges for access to piped water. The higher fees are both a contribution for earlier efforts of other people and a form of anticipatory tax to pay for later costs.

Authorities also note that when new wealthier residents arrive and build larger houses, they bring with them different water use practices. For example, newcomers use piped water to wash cars and cultivate ornamental flower gardens. Wealthier households also can afford to construct large cisterns for storing water. A few households even install swimming pools, which are rarely filled with water because the community has such limited water for basic needs. New residents accustomed to water-intensive practices put pressure on limited water resources and potentially channel limited water away from daily necessities and toward recreational uses. Some authorities think that high water fees might help discourage outsiders from moving to the community and thus limit population pressures on the water system. At the very least, authorities send the message to newcomers that los Purifiqueños take water matters very seriously.

DRINKING WATER CONTRACTS

After paying the required fees, residents receive drinking water contracts for household water connections. Drinking water contracts have a place for residents to indicate by signature that they agree to abide by the community's customs, but the customs are not explicitly described. Similar wording is found in contracts for registering land with the community authorities. The water connection remains in the resident's name and is a right that can be transferred if the resident moves to another property, although this sort of transfer is rare. Usually the drinking water connection is simply sold with the property, which involves another contentious issue in the community. Residents know that the value of land can double or triple if it includes access to piped water. Thus, the community thinks it is fair to charge high fees for a water connection because individuals may install water to personally profit by selling land with water access.

The terms of such water contracts make sense to established residents, even if the implications of the contracts are not explicitly stated. New residents are frustrated that, after paying thousands of pesos for a registered water connection, they must also provide funds for the labor and materials needed to connect their households to the piped water system. Each household must pay for the connection themselves, which costs another few hundred pesos and entails buying materials such as valves, copper and galvanized water pipes, rubber hoses, and spigots, and paying an authorized local plumber to connect the household to the main water lines. Contracts do not state that the use of piped water obligates residents to complete religious mayordomía service when elected. Established residents understand that custom, but newcomers without previous ties to the community are surprised to find out about such obligations unless a local authority explicitly explains this to them beforehand.

WATER FEES

After obtaining authorized connections to the piped water system, household members are also obligated to pay for their water consumption. In 1994 authorities began charging 25 pesos per month or 300 pesos per year. This rate remained in effect until 2003 when the rate was increased to 35 pesos per month or 420 pesos per year. Thus, smaller households of two members may consume less water than larger households of eight members, but both households pay the same water fee. The same water fee applies across households because households do not pay per resident or per volume of water consumed but rather for the guarantee of receiving access to water for a similar minimum amount of time each week. In other words, each household has the potential to access the same volume of water regardless of whether the household consumes that water.

This communal approach guarantees that each household receives sufficient water to meet basic needs, and the rationing system limits overconsumption of water by heavy water users.

Community authorities propose the water fees at annual community assemblies and residents vote to accept or reject the fees. Authorities calculate the water fees mainly based on the total amount of electricity used to run the water pump, so that, in a sense, residents pay primarily for electricity not water. The fees are also based on the estimated costs of maintenance, repair, and improvement of the piped water system.

Various civil administrations have taken into account local economic differences among residents and tried to institute categories for charging for monthly water use. When the water system was first installed in the late 1970s, the community had little need for such categories because most residents had similar-sized houses, similar patterns of water consumption, and similar levels of participation in cooperative labor projects.

New residents—especially upper-income professionals—have moved to the community and have built large permanent houses and weekend vacation homes with large cisterns, personal water pumps, and indoor plumbing for laundry facilities and multiple bathrooms with flush toilets and showers. The wealthier residents also tend to use domestic water rather than irrigation water to maintain lawns and ornamental flower gardens. This sort of water infrastructure is something that smaller households—especially lower-income households—cannot

Figure 5.2 An older adobe house. The house has small windows and an inner courtyard and is surrounded by agricultural land. By 2003, the grandchildren of the original inhabitant no longer relied on agriculture and were in the process of dividing the land to build four new houses for family members.

Figure 5.3 A newer house. The dwelling is constructed with cement bricks and large glass windows and has an inner space for parking cars behind a large locked gate. A tall stone and metal fence surrounds the property, which includes an ornamental garden but no agricultural land. In the foreground, a truck delivers alfalfa for animal feed to other houses. This image illustrates La Purificación's transition from a predominantly rural setting to a more urbanized community.

afford to build, so they rely on the daily supply of water piped to the house. To established residents, it seems obvious that new larger residential houses require more piped water than typical campesino households.

With the support of general community assemblies in the 1990s, the community began instituting four broad categories of water users: (1) regular users with small or average-sized houses were charged 25 pesos per month; (2) owners of rental units were charged 50 to 75 pesos per month; (3) regular users with a large house were charged 75 pesos per month (in some documents this category is referred to as the "rich class"); and (4) owners of unoccupied houses who did not consume water but wanted to maintain their right to a water connection were charged a "half fee" or 12.50 pesos per month.

Water authorities, however, have found this policy to be difficult to enforce. Over time, authorities have ceased using the categories and rather charge the same 25 pesos per month fee for most types of houses. Once a civil authority in one administration grants a lower rate to a resident, it is difficult to change it to a higher rate later, even if the household obviously uses more water than other households. Carlos explained that the changes in administrations every three years provide opportunities for residents to negotiate lower water fees with new water authorities. Changes in water fees were especially likely if a resident had a family member, *compadre,* or neighbor elected to a cargo in the delegación. Because of some of these problems, the community abandoned this fee structure in 2003 and instituted a uniform fee regardless of the size of the house. At the same time, authorities instituted a more strict rationing system for water delivery, further limiting overconsumption and encouraging water conservation.

In addition to monthly water fees, residents are obligated to pay other special user fees for repairs of the piped water system. For instance, during the 1994–1996 administration, the Drinking Water Committee charged every registered water user 110 pesos for repairs of the damaged water pump. Water users are also obligated to attend faenas for piped water projects or, alternatively, pay money or contribute materials toward the project. For example, when the Drinking Water Committee organized a series of faenas to build a new water tank in Barrio de La Concepción, each registered water user was expected to contribute labor for at least three faenas per year for this project. Those who did not complete three faenas were required to pay 35 pesos per faena or provide its equivalent in bags of cement or other materials.

Officials register each water connection in one resident's name. Residents with more than one house may have separate connections registered in their names. Sometimes, authorities encounter problems with this registration system. Residents sometimes use the water in unofficial ways and use one connection for more than one household. This is especially true when grown children stay with their parents and build a separate dwelling on the family property. Some new couples simply extend their water lines with pipes or hoses from their parents' houses to new dwellings without officially registering the separate water connections. Community authorities regard such clandestine water connections as illegal and pressure new couples to register separate water connections for their households.

Water use, of course, is very public. Residents know that each community member relies on community water resources for bathing and drinking. Many residents expect all couples to pay for their consumption of water. In this sense, couples rather than households are the locally recognized social unit for measuring water consumption. Single adult children or unmarried women with children are not expected to pay separate water fees while they live in their parents' households. Elderly parents living with adult children also are not expected to pay separate water fees. The issue of who should pay for water consumption is an ongoing debate at community assemblies, and it is an issue commonly discussed in everyday encounters. Some households that pay 35 pesos per month for water consumption have several married couples and as many as 20 members living on a property with only one official water connection. In community assemblies and other encounters, residents point out that it is not fair that households of two adults with no children pay the same fee as households of two or three couples and their children. Officials say that all couples should be obligated to contribute to the water system, just as all adult men are supposed to fulfill social patrol duty and all property owners are obligated to fulfill cargo service and faenas.

The customary manner of charging for water is a point of contention for new residents who regularly question the relationship between piped water and faenas, fiestas, and family composition. They argue that water consumption ought to be linked to a particular property regardless of how many family members or married couples live on the property. Some new residents suggest that it should not matter how many family members live in the household as long as the registered water user pays the monthly water fee.

Some residents of lower socioeconomic strata cannot pay the required monthly fees to receive piped water. Authorities allow some residents to provide nonmonetary means for fulfilling their obligations. For example, authorities allow residents who are behind in their payments to provide extra labor on repairs and expansion of the piped water system. This helps civil authorities who sometimes need labor to finish projects as much as they need money to purchase construction materials. At times, local plumbers, bricklayers, construction workers, and day laborers work on the water system in exchange for various months of water. In fact, civil authorities note that the community-controlled water system is advantageous in that paying for labor with a few months of water costs less than paying with money. Furthermore, some residents are so poor that officials doubt they will ever be able to afford to pay all of their water fees. What counts is that residents contribute their fair share of a combination of money and labor to maintain the right to piped water. This idea also reflects a long-standing value on providing security for the lower-income members of the community. Local control of the water system allows authorities to provide water security for those households most in need, a practice that would not be possible if water was distributed solely on market principles.

WATER AND COOPERATION

Receiving a household water connection implies that water users must also contribute (*cooperar*) to other customary and traditional practices. A resident who contributes time, money, and labor to the community is referred to by a variety of names, such as a contributor (*cooperador*), someone who pulls their weight (*jalador*), and a hard worker (*chambeador*). A resident who does not contribute is considered a debtor (*moroso*). No codified list of obligations exists for each resident, but rather each resident fulfills customs and traditions in a somewhat flexible manner. According to tradition, residents are expected to contribute to the benefit of the community and, in turn, can expect to receive benefits, with piped water being a major benefit. Residents participate in a wide range of public works projects, including those directly related to piped water. Failure to comply results in the risk of being penalized, including having local authorities physically sever the household's connection to the piped water system.

Civil authorities coordinate numerous faenas each year. During the 1994–1996 administration, some projects were related to the piped water system, including the construction of a new water tank in Barrio de la Concepción and the replacement of damaged water pipes in the colonia. Projects also dealt with other areas of community life, including the construction of a new and larger dam for the irrigation system; the replacement of the irrigation system's dug-earth canals with cement canals to limit leakage; and the improvement of several streets in the community. It is a testimony to the community's customary way of mobilizing resources that the community accomplished these projects during Mexico's national economic crisis that began in 1995. Local

Figure 5.4 Adults and youth working during a faena *to build a new tank for storing water.*

authorities mobilize the system of local leadership with expertise and faenas. They also use local construction materials such as rocks, sand, and community land. These projects involve considerable time, labor, money, and other resources from the entire body of officials in the delegación and the *ejido* as well as residents fulfilling community obligations.

In addition to this work in civil cargos and faenas, residents engage in other forms of nonobligatory, unremunerated community work. For example, volunteers join drinking water commissions that make house-to-house visits requesting payments from water debtors. Community work also includes attending assemblies, assisting in burials in the cemetery, and responding when a resident rings the church bell to alert the community about emergencies such as fires, land invasions, and robberies. Although these tasks are voluntary, and failure to participate does not result in an official penalty, many residents say that not participating "looks bad" and may hurt one's chances to receive similar aid in the future.

MAYORDOMÍA OBLIGATIONS AND WATER

Mayordomía service is a significant expression of cooperation in the community and all property owners are obligated to serve for a year in the mayordomías when called upon. In addition, household members are expected to pay annual contributions to support the fiestas and maintain the church buildings and properties. In 1995, each household paid 168 pesos in an annual contribution. *Mayordomos* also request other residents to contribute to the mayordomías by

Figure 5.5 Installing new religious cargo *officers during a Catholic mass on New Year's Day. The outgoing* mayordomos *and* mayordomas *carry candles, staffs, and keys to the church, which they give to the incoming religious officers.*

accepting smaller cargos such as sponsoring a rosary for one day during the months of May and June, providing a meal during a fiesta, or sponsoring some part of a religious celebration during Christmas or Easter. Officials have decreased the burden of serving in religious cargos by increasing the number of religious cargos in the mayordomías, spreading out the work and cost of the fiesta sponsorship. The community used to elect eight to 10 residents in the mayordomías each year, but starting in the 1990s the community began electing 40 residents as mayordomos and mayordomas each year.

Some residents do not wish to accept religious cargos, so community officials pressure residents to contribute to mayordomía service. The most significant pressure involves threatening to shut off a household's piped water connection. For example, in 1995 many households struggled with the economic crisis and did not want the economic burden of sponsoring the upcoming annual festivals. In meetings between civil and religious authorities, residents elected for the 1996 mayordomías said that it was not fair for a few families to take on this burden. Residents said they would not accept the cargos in the mayordomías if community authorities did not obligate those residents appearing next on the roster to also accept cargos in the mayordomías. They argued that everyone would benefit from and enjoy the masses, dances, music, fireworks, and meals, so everyone should cooperate in this community custom and provide religious cargo service when elected.

Eventually, to pressure residents, civil and religious authorities held a community assembly on December 31, 1995, and passed a resolution to have civil authorities shut off the piped water supply of households that did not accept religious cargo service in the mayordomías. By early January 1996, 40 men and women accepted the religious cargos in time to start organizing the annual cycle of religious fiestas, which began with plans for the community's largest fiesta, including the celebration of the community's patron on February 2. A few other residents signed agreements with civil and religious authorities promising to serve in 1997 if they could be exempt from service in 1996.

A few months later, religious authorities pressured the civil authorities to abide by the resolutions passed at the community assembly. In the summer of 1996, mayordomos and mayordomas accompanied civil authorities to various households to warn residents with water debts that their piped water would be shut off. At the same time, they also warned debtor households that they also needed to be up to date in their obligatory annual religious offerings (*limosnas*) for the fiestas or risk having their piped water shut off. In other words, the religious officers reminded households that they were expected to pay both civil and religious fees or risk civil authorities imposing the same sanction.

Most established residents accept and support the blending of civil and religious matters as part of the local system of *usos y costumbres*. Members of the Drinking Water Committee also accept this blending and suggest that it benefits the community because it helps pressure residents to pay drinking water fees. In 1996, when religious authorities went house to house to collect contributions for fiestas, they told residents who did not pay that the mayordomos and mayordomas had the authority to shut off the household's piped water. After hearing such threats, residents paid their drinking water debts to lessen the risk that their water would be shut off. These examples show how local control of water helps reinforce other aspects of traditional culture that national government policy tends to ignore and criticize.

THE CEMETERY AND COOPERATION

The cemetery holds a special place in community life and figures in local struggles over drinking water. The cemetery symbolizes community identity, because, as residents reminded me more than once, "we all go there sooner or later." The cemetery is the community's only local place to bury the dead. In addition, the cemetery serves as the space for holding the annual Day of the Dead ceremonies that occur November 1 and 2. With small monuments to honor community residents, the cemetery is a place for family to place flowers on their relatives' graves on special days, such as Easter, a patron saint's day, and anniversary dates of births or deaths.

In conversations, residents frequently discuss drinking water in connection to the cemetery when talking about community customs. When urging authorities to impose a sanction on residents who refuse to serve in civil and religious cargos, residents often say that authorities should shut off the household's drinking water connection and deny debtors access to the cemetery. Residents who fulfilled their community contributions, on the other hand, expect to receive plots to bury dead family members, and they count on receiving help to bury the dead.

Figure 5.6 Digging a grave in the local cemetery during the annual Day of the Dead ceremony on November 2.

These issues emerge each Sunday when mayordomos and mayordomas collect household contributions for the fiestas. When I accompanied them during their house-to-house collections, I noticed that some nonresidents from cities visiting kin on the weekend donated money to support the fiestas and received written receipts. Some visitors told me that although they do not live in La Purificación, they contribute to the fiestas as well as projects dealing with drinking water, the schools, and road construction. They usually keep a stack of receipts to support the claim that "I have cooperated with the community," which can be useful for the day when their kin requests burial rights for them in the community cemetery.

In contrast, I was present in the delegacíon when some families with histories of not contributing to the community sought to bury a dead relative. The families quickly learned that they had to pay civil authorities a sum of money, thousands of pesos, or look for an alternative cemetery. Even in matters of death, fulfilling community obligations defines one's place in the community.

Alternatives for burying the dead are not appealing. Many residents avoid what they called ugly or *feo* public cemeteries in Texcoco and Mexico City. Public cemeteries charge substantial fees to bury a body and use the grave for seven years, the time given for the body to decompose. Unless the family pays a perpetual fee every seven years, cemetery officials will dig up the body, scatter the bones, remove the grave marker with the person's name, and use the grave to bury the body of an unrelated person. Residents worry that this ugly, impersonal burial means that dead relatives will be abandoned and forgotten.

Nancy Scheper-Hughes (1992) refers to similar burials in poorer urban areas of Brazil as forms of everyday violence.

Los Purifiqueños seek to avoid this sort of violence. In contrast to views of urban cemeteries, los Purifiqueños view their community's cemetery as a respectable burial place, not a place to buy and sell plots. A family can bury a body in a grave and, after seven years, bury another dead relative in the same plot, but they place grave markers for each dead family member. No one is forgotten. The cemetery expresses social bonds and mutual support between citizen and community, and it provides a meaningful space for families to remember the dead. Indeed, whenever I return to La Purificación, I visit the graves of friends who have died since I began my ethnographic studies of the community.

Officers in the civil–religious hierarchy make major decisions regarding access to cemetery plots and burial rights. Mayordomos and mayordomas, not the priest or other religious official, give and deny families permission to use the church for burial mass and to toll the church bell on the day of the person's death as well as the day of the funeral. The church bells call residents to gather to help the dead person's family by praying, consoling grieving relatives, and bringing food to the house of the deceased. The bells also call men to assist the family in digging a cemetery plot, which is a laborious task usually involving a group of 10 or more men with their own picks and shovels to dig for hours in the rocky soil. Some residents refer to this work as a faena, although community authorities do not officially regard such work as fulfilling faena obligations. This meaningful work, however, contributes to the larger web of mutual support provided in a close-knit community.

Mayordomos and maryordomas can also recommend that civil authorities not assign a burial plot to someone until the family is up to date in paying fees related to mayordomía service or festival sponsorship. Civil authorities give families permission to use burial plots, and someone from the Citizen's Participation Council accompanies family members, often exclusively men, to assign a burial plot. Officers do not charge residents for a burial plot, but they do verify that members of the household of the dead person are current in their community contributions—fees related to faenas, social patrol duties, and drinking water bills—before assigning a burial plot. Authorities do not like taking these measures. Speaking of such cases, Carlos, the president of the Drinking Water Committee, said, "It is sad." But, he added, "it is the only way" to pressure residents into fulfilling their obligations.

Death of a family member is a moment when households become involved in the community's practices of cooperation. Officers of the civil–religious hierarchy manage central activities surrounding burial and express a dead person's social ties to the community. Authorities grant access to cemetery plots and, in a sense, open access to community resources to residents who have participated in and worked for the benefit of the larger community. On the other hand, authorities close community resources to those who have not cooperated. Death of a family member is a poignant moment, and the community controls crucial resources involved in death customs. This sort of closure of community resources has long been an important aspect of maintaining strong campesino communities in Mexico (Roseberry 1989; Wolf 1955, 1986, 1990).

Contributing to drinking water development helps ensure one's place in the community and that one will receive ultimately a proper burial in La Purificación. Issues of death and religion involve practices of cooperation and illustrate that drinking water is embedded in a larger symbolic field of community life. In effect, connection to drinking water symbolizes a social bond one has with other residents engaged in activities that have a collective benefit. Individuals have a right to benefit from community resources—drinking water, the church, emergency assistance, and respectable burial sites—as long as they also contribute to the community.

When analyzing cooperation, I do not mean to suggest that los Purifiqueños impose cemetery policies only because they are useful for managing the drinking water system. Rather, the efforts of residents fit within a broader web of principles, values, and practices that they use to orient their lives. Similar principles of reciprocity shape a variety of personal relationships involving kinship, friends, meals, and public and private fiestas. Los Purifiqueños note that being good neighbors and living with others (*convivir*) entails strong social bonds and reciprocity. In this sense, practices of cooperation are not valued because they are useful for managing drinking water, but rather, because they maintain egalitarian resource principles. As a result, the practices shape the course of drinking water management. Culture, indeed, deeply impacts how residents handle their precious liquid.

DEBT AND DEBTORS

The ways residents talk about debtors reflects the local conception of rights and obligations. Officials told me about some of the residents who receive adequate water but who have not fulfilled their obligations to contribute money and labor for community projects. Los Purifiqueños use the term *moroso* to refer to people who have not paid their water fees. This was especially evident to me during a two-week period in 1995 when the community's water supply was suspended after the electric company shut off electricity to run the water pump (see Chapter 7). Mexico's national economic crisis made it difficult for many residents to pay water fees, leaving the Drinking Water Committee without sufficient funds to pay electric fees to run the community's water pump. Residents understood the difficulty everyone was having with the crisis, but they referred to households that owed more than one year of water fees as debtors (*morosos*), delinquents (*gente morosa*), and lazy or negligent (*desidioso*). These sorts of labels were part of a process of shaming residents to pressure them to fulfill their obligations. Such terms refer to debts involving money as well as debts involving participation in collective life, and contrast with the notion of cooperation (*cooperación*). Community residents commonly refer to those who do not contribute to any cooperative labor projects as parasites (*parásitos*) and selfish (*egoísta*). Residents also apply the same terms to individuals who refuse to fulfill service in civil or religious cargos. In this sense, los Purifiqueños are referring to a resident's social debt.

SHUTTING OFF WATER

Community authorities maintain the right to shut off drinking water from debtors who fail to fulfill community obligations, especially those who fail to complete civil or religious cargo service. In community assemblies and in encounters in civil offices, community residents, including former office holders, pressure civil authorities to apply such sanctions to debtors. The imposition of the sanction involves physically severing a household's water connection from the main water lines. Authorities also ask neighbors not to give water to the household.

During my stays in La Purificación, I often heard residents request that authorities shut off a debtor's drinking water, but I rarely observed the application of this sanction. One reason is that most residents comply with major obligations, so there is little need to apply the sanction. Also, unlike urban facilities, household water connections in La Purificación do not have valves and meters that authorities can turn off and lock. Authorities physically have to sever a household's water connection and remove pipes that lead to the main water network. This process is difficult, costly, and, as I point out below, legally risky for the community. When authorities do shut off drinking water connections, they tend to target a few households as a way to shame a few individuals and thus send a quick message for others to comply. Such examples show other residents that the threat of this sanction is a real possibility, so most pay their debts to avoid going without piped water as well as to avoid the public shaming associated with water cut offs.

I followed up on cases from years past to examine the complicated application of this sanction. After having their drinking water shut off, people have used the legal system to argue that community authorities committed a crime. According to federal law, drinking water from underground sources is a national good, and access to water is listed as a constitutional guarantee for all Mexican citizens (Leyes y Códigos de México 1994a, 1994b). Lawyers have counseled local authorities that, when they shut off a household's drinking water, they risk being criminally charged with the crime of abuse of power. Municipio of Texcoco authorities have arrested community authorities and jailed them for a few days in Texcoco for this crime. Such cases appear to involve local authorities pressuring individuals to conform to community customs not related directly to drinking water obligations, such as shutting off drinking water for someone who refuses to fulfill mayordomía service. Community officials said that Texcoco authorities allow the community to shut off a household's drinking water supply if the household has a substantial monetary debt involving its drinking water account. In fact, according to officials in Texcoco, city officials do the same thing. Lawyers have suggested to authorities in La Purificación that, rather than completely shutting off water, they should restrict water "to a trickle" (*por goteo*) to allow the household a minimum amount of drinking water for vital needs and to comply with minimum legal standards. Lawyers suggest that authorities take this course of action even in cases of residents who owe several years of water fees.

My observations of several cases of water shutoffs also indicate the complexity of applying this sanction. I observed authorities shutting off drinking water of households with two or more years of not paying drinking water fees. This involved sending several written notices to households stating that they risked having their water shut off, and summoning debtors to the delegación to inform them of the problem. Sometimes authorities went to debtor households as a group of eight to 10 men comprising delegados, representatives from the Drinking Water Committee and other civil committees, representatives from the ejido, and plumbers. Other times, representatives of the mayordomías and from a voluntary citizen's drinking water commission joined the civil authorities. When the entire group arrived at several households, group members informed household members that they were delinquent on their water payments and that the group would be shutting off the household's drinking water supply. In a few instances, debtors gave officials money to cover part of the water debt and promised to pay the balance within a specified time. In most instances, however, the group dug up the water line, used a hacksaw to sever the intake water pipe leading to the household, and installed a clamp on the water connection. Authorities notified household members that they could receive water after they paid for past due water fees and for the materials and the labor of the plumber to shut off and reconnect the water supply. The imposition of sanctions seemed to be effective because most debtor households promptly paid their debts. Other debtors, upon hearing about these cases, also arrived at civil offices to pay debts and avoid the imposition of sanctions, not to mention the shame they feel when a group of neighbors appears on the doorstep with pickaxes, hacksaws, and shovels in hand.

Figure 5.7 Civil officers and volunteers of the citizens' drinking water commission disconnect a household water connection.

COOPERATION

Los Purifiqueños rely on many cooperative practices to manage drinking water as a communal resource. Authorities distribute a sufficient minimum amount of drinking water to all households and expect residents to pay money as well as contribute labor in the form of cargo service, faenas, fiesta participation, and other forms of mutual aid. These practices relate to power struggles over local policies and practices, such as the differential categories for water connections and sanctions for lack of community participation. These practices may look new, but many residents regard such practices as consistent with traditional views of water as a communal resource. Campesino life in La Purificación has been changed by a market economy, in-migration, population increases, and a growing importance placed on water for household consumption rather than for irrigation. Nevertheless, nonmarket mechanisms, such as kinship and residency status, mediate drinking water distribution and somewhat limit the pressure to use market-based distribution principles that would supply water to residents based on payment of money for the amounts consumed.

Community control of drinking water concentrates power in a few individuals who obligate other community residents to engage in an assortment of customary activities. For many residents, the benefits of a fair distribution of drinking water offset the coercive effects of drinking water management. Many residents abide by community customs and relinquish some individual autonomy as long as they and their family members receive a fair share of community resources. For the time being, community values of fairness, reciprocity, and cooperation prevail in this water system.

6/"Everything Is the Responsibility of the Woman"
Gender and Water Management

When I first visited La Purificación in 1993, I learned that no woman had ever served on the Drinking Water Committee. This was not an unusual finding. Ethnographic research in the northern Acolhuacan region and elsewhere in the Valley of Mexico suggested that traditional gender differentiation had limited women's participation in civil and religious *cargos*. Indeed, after completing the initial phases of my research, I reported similar findings noting that women in La Purificación had begun to be elected to religious cargos but not civil cargos (Ennis-McMillan 2001b). Women's participation in *mayordomías* was changing and influencing water issues, but only men occupied the formal civil positions of authority over La Purificación's piped water system. This fits a general pattern throughout rural, peri-urban, and urban communities in the Valley of Mexico, where men tend to be elected as public water administrators. Culture, however, is always a dynamic and ever-changing process, so I should have expected to encounter new twists to the anthropological puzzle about water and tradition in La Purificación.

I returned to La Purificación to conduct summer fieldwork in 2002, and when I walked into the *delegación* offices I saw Aurora sitting behind the Drinking Water Committee desk. Her face lit up and she said, "Hola Michael! What a miracle!" I appreciated Aurora's exuberant greeting, which was a common response from los Purifiqueños who had not seen me in a couple of years. Aurora is a retired schoolteacher and a widow with an adult son and daughter who are raising children of their own. I had known Aurora's family for years, and I was glad to see her. But I was surprised to see a woman sitting behind the Drinking Water Committee desk. I asked myself whether Aurora's presence was a one-time event for the day or in fact a shift in cargos.

After Aurora and I hugged, I asked in a joking manner, "Don't tell me they put you in charge of the water?" Aurora laughed and replied, "Yes, can you believe it?" Aurora explained that she and two other women had been elected to the Drinking Water Committee. Her sister, too, had been elected to a civil cargo on the Citizen's Participation Council. I told Aurora that I had just published a

*Figure 6.1 Aurora (second from right) sits at the Drinking Water Committee desk as a
civil cargo officer.*

book in Spanish where I reported that women in La Purificación do not hold civil
cargos in the delegación (Ennis-McMillan 2001b). "Well," Aurora said, "You
will have to do more research." I agreed, and thus began a new phase of my studies of los Purifiqueños and their water customs.

After completing further research that summer and the next, I better understood that the ongoing transformations in the civil–religious cargo system have
opened up new opportunities for women to have a more direct influence on
water management. Women often have the primary responsibility for managing
precious water resources within the household, but their increasing participation
in water management outside the household extends rather than departs from traditional gender expectations. In La Purificación, women actively participate in
activities that ensure that water is distributed equitably to all households that pay
user fees and fulfill customary labor obligations. As part of this process women
are being elected to the community's Drinking Water Committee and other civil
and religious cargos previously held only by men.

WOMEN AND WATER IN LA PURIFICACIÓN

Until 2000, only men were elected to civil cargos, including those dealing
directly with managing the piped water system and overseeing the surface water
for irrigation and household use. When the piped water system was installed in
the late 1970s, men managed the system and most registered household connections in their names, just as they had with irrigation water. Up until that time,
most households relied on agricultural production and were male-headed. Men

also traditionally took care of water matters outside the house, such as paying water fees at the municipal offices. Few water accounts were listed under a woman's name.

In 1980, the first year that piped household water connections were registered, 100 households out of a total of about 250 households had piped water connections. The households without piped water continued to rely on the surface water for both irrigation and household consumption. Of the first 100 households to register piped water connections, 16 accounts were listed under women, most of whom were widows, divorcees, or daughters of elderly parents. All 16 of these women were long-term residents living in extended families whose income relied on a mixture of agriculture and wage labor.

By 1996, 865 households registered piped water connections, of which 257 accounts (nearly one-third of the total) were listed under a woman's name. These figures reflect growth in the number of female-headed households as well as a combination of other factors, including a persistent view of women as managers of household water and new economic opportunities for women in the region. An increasing number of women, both new and established residents, travel by bus and car each day to work in Texcoco and other nearby cities.

These women have the ability to establish and maintain their own households in the community. In some cases, daughters with income from wage work have inherited family property formerly used for agriculture and built separate houses. In other cases, women have moved from Texcoco and Mexico City to establish their own households in La Purificación. Widowed and divorced women are also listed in the Drinking Water Committee's account books as the heads of households. Still other cases involve daughters whose aging parents transferred the household's water connection to their names and locally born women who inherited family property and live with husbands not native to the community. Regarding this latter case, Carlos, the president of the Drinking Water Committee, explained that these women—as established residents—usually register the water connections in their names because they are eligible for the lower household connection fee. He also noted that some households register the irrigation water account in the men's names and the piped water account in the women's names because women are more likely to be in charge of household water-related tasks. As registered users of the piped water, women have become active in the management of the water in ways that were not apparent in the earlier management of surface water.

One of my good friends, Carmen, was particularly active in water issues. During an extended interview, I asked Carmen why she and other women participated in drinking water issues. She offered the following explanation:

> Water probably interests us [women] more [than men] because we use it in everything, yes for everything. The man does not care. He just takes a bath and leaves and that's it. And not so with the woman, because the woman knows that everything, everything, everything in life that she does in the house is about water, is done with water. If we are going to bathe, if we are going to wash our hands, if we are going to wash a diaper, if we are going to prepare some tea, if we are going to wash a baby's bottle, everything, everything, everything is the responsibility of the woman.

Figure 6.2 Carmen (right) working during a faena *with other women. The* facna *was part of an ongoing project to build a new water tank for the western half of the community. Carmen is accompanied by her sister, an aunt, and neighbors.*

The following sections introduce Carmen and describe her participation in La Purificación's water system. Focusing on one woman's experiences illustrates the dynamic process by which other women have become involved in local water issues. Carmen's story reflects broader community trends regarding gender and water management.

CARMEN'S HOUSEHOLD

Carmen has resided in La Purificación most of her life. She was born in the 1940s, and fondly recalls her days as a child when the pueblo had a population under 1,000 residents. She completed six years of primary school in the community. As a young single woman, she worked in a garment factory in Mexico City for seven years, but later returned home. Her father, now deceased, was an established resident, and her mother is from a nearby state. When Carmen was growing up, her family relied on a mixture of wage labor and limited subsistence agriculture. They lived near the center of the community, in Barrio de Santa Teresa, just south of the church and the main plaza. The family property consisted of agricultural land of more than 3,000 square meters, on which they used irrigation water for growing crops and for domestic purposes.

Over the years, Carmen's father divided his property among his adult children so that they all had places to settle with their own families. In the 1970s, Carmen married Jorge, who was also born in the community, and they built a one-story house on a roughly 300-square-meter plot of land that her father sold

Figure 6.3 Carmen's family. Four generations live in an extended family compound.

her. Her modest house was constructed of cement blocks, glass windows, and a cement floor and roof. Later, Carmen and Jorge added a second story of rooms for their two daughters and son. The house has electricity and telephone service, and Carmen owns two televisions and a car. In addition to raising three children, Carmen and her husband raised two nieces and a nephew who are children of Carmen's deceased sister. In the last few years, Carmen and her husband have had marital problems and have separated and reunited a few times.

Like other established families, Carmen lives in an extended family compound of four generations, consisting of her household and three other households. The families in the compound collectively consist of about 20 individuals. All the households pool resources for some activities, such as buying food for family celebrations and cooking in a common kitchen. Carmen's mother owns the family's original house, which is located in the center of the property. Carmen's sister and three of her four children also live in this house. Carmen's house is in the front part of the property where she and Jorge live with the youngest niece as well as their son, his wife, and their child. Carmen's two daughters have married and moved to adjoining communities, and each has a child. In the back of the family compound, Carmen's two brothers live in separate houses with their respective wives and children.

Although Carmen refers to her family as *campesinos,* they no longer rely on agricultural production for their livelihood. With only a few remaining apple and peach trees, the family has converted the agricultural land into smaller residential plots and they no longer receive irrigation water. Carmen works at home, and her daughters provide her with some support. In recent years, she converted a bedroom into a small convenience store to sell candy, soda pop, snacks, soap,

Figure 6.4 Interviewing a mayordoma *and her family about water issues in La Purificación. I tape-recorded the interview and used an open-ended questionnaire to elicit information.*

and other small items. She also sews garments on a piecework basis for a merchant in the region, and her husband works as a mechanic in Texcoco. Carmen's siblings work outside of the community. Her sister is a seamstress in a garment factory, one brother is a prison guard, and the other brother is a technician at a nearby agricultural college. Carmen's children have begun careers as business and legal professionals, and her nieces and nephews attend postsecondary schools.

Within the extended family compound, each household has its own separate connection to the community's piped water system and each household pays its own water fees. Carmen's household water connection is registered in her name and not Jorge's because she bought the property from her father and pays for many of the household expenses, especially when they have marital difficulties and he returns to his natal home.

The household has a typical water delivery and storage system. As with most houses in the community, Carmen's house does not have a cistern, but it has a rooftop tank with a capacity of about 130 gallons. Carmen also stores water in a large 50-gallon plastic container in the bathroom and a few 6-gallon plastic buckets. In addition, the family compound stores water in an outdoor 500-gallon *pileta,* which is a rectangular concrete water reservoir where the women do laundry and wash dishes. Thus, Carmen's residence has the capacity to store about 200 gallons of water per day for use in the house, and she has access to the water in the compound's pileta. Wastewater from the indoor bathroom and sinks drains into a septic tank, but gray wastewater from the laundry drains onto the property.

Carmen usually fills the household's water reservoirs on the days they receive water, which usually occurs every other day between 9:00 A.M. and 11:00 A.M. Because water runs every other day, the household has the capacity to store about 30 gallons of water per person for use inside the house over two days. As in many households, the women in Carmen's extended family wash clothes, clean dishes, and complete other household chores at the same time the water is being delivered to the house and filling water reservoirs. In this manner, the water reservoirs remain full and the four households have plenty of water stored at later times for bathing, cooking, and other activities.

Carmen's views on water quality are typical of other residents. When I asked Carmen if she was concerned about the quality of the drinking water, she replied, "No," and added that she was more worried that the groundwater was becoming depleted (that is, the water table was falling) and that the community's water pump was aging and having more mechanical problems. Carmen said she could not recall anyone in her family ever having a health problem from drinking the piped water. Carmen said that she and her family members usually drink water directly from the tap and rarely boil water before drinking it, unless they boil water to make coffee or tea. I also asked Carmen if she used irrigation water for domestic purposes. She said she grew up drinking the irrigation water, but she said she would no longer do so because the irrigation water had become dirty (*sucia*) from people throwing garbage and sewage into the irrigation canals. In Carmen's view, the benefits of having adequate piped water make it worthwhile to engage in all sorts of water-related work.

WOMEN'S WATER INTERESTS

Regardless of the name on the household water connection, women and girls typically perform most household chores that depend on water. Women also carry out water-related responsibilities such as filling piletas, barrels, and buckets, allocating water for domestic chores, rationing water during shortages, and making sure the household's monthly water fees are paid. Women truly are the managers of water within the house.

Women are also the ones most likely to go personally to the civil offices to pay water fees and discuss water distribution problems with civil authorities, who are also often the women's kin, neighbors, or friends. Women regularly notify civil cargo holders of leaks in the main water pipes, improper use of water by other residents, and the failure of piped water to reach the house on time or in the allotted amount.

Furthermore, women link their interest in household water use with the public administration of the piped water system through specific public activities. Now that more women like Carmen have the household water connections listed in their names, they join men in contributing *faena* labor for drinking water projects. As Carmen and others pointed out to me, an increasing number of women have the same community obligations as men because more have income and property as a result of the region's expanding wage-labor economy. In some cases, access to wage jobs has allowed a greater number of women to gain water rights, which obligates them to fulfill faenas. For irrigation projects, I observed

Figure 6.5 Washing dishes outside in a pileta. *While visiting La Purificación, my mother (right) learned how to make tamales. The women use the water in the* pileta *to prepare food, and wash dishes and clothes.*

men exclusively engaging in faenas. By contrast, at several faenas for developing the drinking water system, I observed women and girls working alongside men hauling rocks, digging ditches, coordinating work groups, cleaning large water tanks, and laying water pipes.

One summer, for example, Carmen, her aunt, her sister, and several other women joined approximately 50 men in a series of faenas to build a new large water tank in the eastern half of the community. For several Saturday mornings volunteers hauled rocks from the mountainside down to the place where a new water storage tank was going to be constructed. Carmen told me that she attended the faena partly to shame the men who did not fulfill their communal labor obligations. From Carmen's point of view, men's lack of involvement in the water system put the entire system at risk. She also said that as a head of her household, it was her obligation to complete faena labor. Other women, too, attended labor projects to install new pipes into sections of the drinking water system. Many women commented that as household heads and those responsible for household water, they had to perform this work even if others thought it was work typically performed by men. Residents explained that all households, including those headed by a widowed or divorced woman, had to fulfill these

Figure 6.6 Women and men working during a faena *to dig a trench for new water pipes.*

labor obligations or risk having local authorities fine them and even cut off their household's water connection.

In addition, women are active in water politics. In interviews and conversations, women and men suggested that because women take a major responsibility for managing household water, they are likely to speak out in public settings and take action on water-related issues outside the household. In addition to completing faenas, women increasingly work as auxiliary civil officers to ensure fair distribution and fulfillment of monetary and labor obligations. They regularly vocalize concerns and attend community assemblies, reminding themselves and others that they have the primary responsibility for completing household tasks that require water. For example, at assemblies in 1995 during the economic crisis, women described the suffering they endured because of water shortages, which prevented them from washing clothes, feeding their families, and cleaning their households (see Chapter 7). Carmen and other women reminded those at the assemblies *"El agua es la vida del pueblo"* or "water is the life of the pueblo".

At the community's first emergency assembly to deal with the water shortage, Carmen and a few other women stood up and spoke of their "suffering from water." Male civil authorities told the assembly of a couple hundred men and women that the drinking water authorities planned to increase their efforts to send written notices to debtors requesting overdue water fees within the next week. Not satisfied with this solution, Carmen and other women stood up on the floor of the assembly and called for an immediate confrontation with debtors. Women prompted the civil authorities in charge of the meeting to immediately

Figure 6.7 Women in a community assembly about water. In the background, the picture on the left is of the man who helped La Purificación secure rights to a portion of the surface water in the 1920s.

form a voluntary water commission. When the assembly finished, the civil authorities formed a water commission composed of male civil authorities and male and female volunteers. Immediately after the assembly, the commission made house-to-house visits, requesting that residents pay water fees to help the community cover the electric bill for the water pump.

The commission collected money that first day, but the commission had to continue pressuring debtors several more times in subsequent months. Commission members threatened and actually disconnected water connections of a few residents with large water debts. At subsequent community assemblies in 1995, Carmen was one of the residents who continued to strongly pressure civil authorities and the water commission to collect from debtors or disconnect debtor households from the water system.

I accompanied Carmen and others as they asked delinquent residents to pay their household drinking water debts. Sometimes the women in the commission scolded men from debtor households and teased by saying they saw the men walking around the pueblo bathed and wearing clean clothes. The joking seemed to be something women did more than men, and offered a less confrontational way to address debtors. The women said it was obvious that the men used the community's water and ought to pay the water fees. Carmen and her aunt explained to debtors that the drinking water cost a household about one peso a day. Carmen was always quick to tell debtors that they wasted more than one peso a day purchasing makeup, beer, and other unnecessary items. As a result of the pressure the commission exerted and the residents' need for domestic water, many households paid their water fees within two weeks, which enabled the community to pay the electric company and restore water service. Women, in these instances, do not hold officially designated civil cargos, but they carry out the vital duties in conjunction with drinking water officials.

GENDER, WATER, AND RELIGIOUS CARGO SERVICE

Local cultural values and practices regarding water management are particularly influential in how the community's traditional *usos y costumbres* link local water issues to cargo service. Recall that at a community assembly soon after the piped water system was installed in the late 1970s, the community members voted to require that all households connected to the piped water system fulfill civil and religious cargo obligations when it was their turn. Carlos, Carmen, and other cargo holders explained that, in accordance with local custom, it was only fair to require civil and religious cargo service from all households who benefited from the community's water.

The change in the selection of cargo officers brought about by the installation of the piped water system set in motion a process whereby women eventually began to be elected to cargos. When changes in election procedures were first instituted, the possibility of electing women to cargos did not seem to have entered into the discussion. Nevertheless, a few women were elected to lower-ranking religious cargos soon after the change was instituted in the 1980s, and over time an increasing number of women have occupied both religious and civil cargos. The increasing participation of women in both religious and civil cargos seems to be an unintended consequence of emphasizing equitable procedures for selecting people for cargo service.

Carmen has been a long-time participant in the mayordomías. In 1973, after building their house, Carmen and Jorge were named to a mayordomía. At the time, they used irrigation water, which was listed in her father's name. Carmen, however, was named as the mayordoma because the house and property were listed in her name. Both she and her husband contributed money and labor to fulfill the obligations of the religious office, but she was the religious officer not Jorge.

In December 1995, Carmen's household again appeared on the rotation schedule for the mayordomías to organize and sponsor the annual religious festivals for 1996. This time, Carmen was separated from Jorge, so she was named to a cargo as an individual resident. The previous religious cargo holders elected Carmen and her brother Raúl to head the mayordomía. Carmen as *fiscala* and her brother Raúl as *fiscal* were coheads of the Mayordomía del Pueblo, the group responsible for the community's largest fiesta on February 2. All the members of the four households in the family compound worked with Carmen and her brother to sponsor and organize the fiesta.

Figure 6.8 Women elected to serve in religious cargos *as* mayordomas. *In the picture, the women collect church donations on a Sunday morning. The church's bell tower rises in the background.*

It is quite common to name two coheads to share the burden of organizing the fiestas and coordinating the work of the other religious officers. Most often two men from the same extended family compound, such as two brothers, two brothers-in-law, two cousins, or an uncle and nephew, are named as coheads. In this way, people share the burdens and responsibilities that go along with the top cargos and use kinship ties to pool resources and facilitate cooperation.

A few times since the 1980s, women have been named to the top religious cargos as fiscalas. In these cases, each woman was paired with a brother, just as Carmen was paired with her brother. In one case a daughter and father carried out a cargo together. In all these cases, the women were established residents who were familiar with community customs.

Another change in the cargo system involved increasing the number of religious cargo officers elected each year from eight to 40. According to community authorities, electing more people to the religious cargos became necessary because the population was increasing and festival sponsorship was becoming too burdensome. Over time, with an increasing number of religious posts to fill and a greater number of women registered as heads of household, the candidates for a particular year increasingly came from female-headed households. Since the 1990s, in any given year, women have occupied a third to a half of the religious cargos.

When I inquired whether opposition had surfaced to electing women to religious cargos, some residents told me that opposition always follows a change in cargo customs. Some residents oppose naming women to these top religious posts, saying that tradition prohibits women from carrying out some obligations of the post, such as being on the altar to assist the priest during a mass. Some also claim that men in lesser offices would not listen to women in the top cargos and that women do not have the physical strength needed to organize the fiestas. However, nobody could recall any major or sustained opposition to naming women to religious cargos. The notion of having a selection system that is *parejo* seems to have overshadowed concerns about traditional gendered notions of cargo service. Furthermore, increasing the number of religious cargos has meant that women could participate with rather than replace men. Despite limited opposition, Carmen and other women are being elected to religious cargos, entering public office within the civil–religious hierarchy, and influencing community issues, particularly issues related to managing scarce water resources.

Carmen and her brother, however, were reluctant to accept the top religious cargos. In late 1995 during the economic crisis, several households turned down religious cargo service and sought to avoid the monetary expenses and labor obligations that accompany sponsoring religious festivals. After accepting her cargo, Carmen coordinated efforts among civil and religious authorities to pressure other residents to accept religious offices in the future. She first organized several meetings among the other religious office holders and led discussions about the need to cut off water to some households. Then she organized special community meetings with civil cargo holders and led discussions about how the community should deal with the issue. The religious cargo holders demanded that the civil authorities threaten to impose sanctions for failure to fulfill mayordomía service. Civil officials agreed to support the religious officers and threaten to disconnect the water of households, especially those of wealthier residents who did not fulfill mayordomía obligations.

As a fiscala, Carmen also continued the work that she had started with the water commissions the summer before. Carmen organized mayordomos and mayordomas to accompany civil authorities in more water commissions in 1996. In this way, the group confronted water debtors as well as residents who refused to accept religious cargos in the mayordomías. Most times, this resulted in households paying all or part of their water debts. A few times, however, a group of 15 to 20 people went to specific houses and disconnected their water supplies. In an extended interview, I asked Carmen why the community took such actions, and she replied as follows:

> There are people with resources, with large houses, which probably have more water because, if you have noticed, they have [ornamental] gardens, patios, and cars that they wash with drinking water, right? Then precisely these people are the ones that have not wanted to collaborate (*colaborar*) by doing their mayordomía . . . . We don't have any other measure except [to shut off] the water, which is the life here of the pueblo.

Carmen criticized people who did not "cooperate with the community" (*cooperar con la comunidad*) by performing community labor in the form of faenas and civil and religious cargo service. She said, "To have these [water] rights, you have to contribute" money and labor to the community. She continued saying, "people pay [money] for one month of water, but they don't do their work." Carmen pointed out that the water fees are relatively low. She explained that ordering a water truck from Texcoco would cost about 80 to 100 pesos for 200 gallons of water, which would not last a week in a typical household. By contrast, households pay 35 pesos per month and receive piped water at least every other day, which is sufficient to meet basic needs. By the economics alone, Carmen thought that it was reasonable to expect all residents to provide community labor to development projects in addition to paying water fees.

I asked Carmen why she supported efforts to shut off water to pressure residents to fulfill obligations related to religious cargos. She explained that it was important for all the authorities to be united. Carmen views her activities as a continuation of a history of her family's participation in community development, which often included the difficult tasks of confronting powerful local families and petitioning government officials for funds and technical assistance for all sorts of development projects. Carmen reminded me that earlier generations of her family had worked together to establish the kindergarten and primary school, build the main paved road, and install the drinking water system. In her view, this unity allowed the community to obtain resources for many other projects: the soccer field, irrigation water, *ejido* improvements, and a government milk distribution program for lower-income households. These past efforts, she said, required the whole community to work together, which is why she supports measures that bring together civil and religious officials to deal with drinking water issues. In Carmen's view, everyone should work as a single team (*un solo equipo*). She reminded me that civil and religious officials work together to hold dances, organize religious processions, and respond to the church bell in the case of emergencies. "It is one branch (*una sola rama*)," she said, emphasizing that unity helps to sustain community life.

ELECTING WOMEN TO THE DRINKING WATER COMMITTEE

In contrast to religious cargos, changes in the election process for civil cargos came about more slowly and women were not immediately elected. The community continued to elect only men from established families to the higher-ranking civil cargos. This election pattern seems related to traditional gender norms that tend to equate men with public leadership positions. Nevertheless, the entrance of women in lower religious cargos of the civil–religious hierarchy eventually led to women occupying higher civil cargos with direct responsibility over water management. By the year 2000, when it came time for the election to civil posts, many candidates were women who had previously participated in the cargo system as religious officers.

Thus, a new generation of women began entering local public office in 2000; they were elected to nine of the 34 civil cargos in the delegación, with seven of

Figure 6.9 Women as members of the Drinking Water Committee. Behind the desk, two women and one man collect water fees and manage the accounts. The older man (seated right) is paying his water fees. The other man (standing right) is a local plumber who installs household water connections and repairs leaks. Local elementary students gave the Drinking Water Committee the poster on the wall, which has figures of large blue water drops and provides information about not wasting water.

these posts assigned to the 18-member Drinking Water Committee. Before 2000, the Drinking Water Committee consisted of seven positions, but the community voted to expand the number from seven to 18 because of the community population growth. In the 2000–2003 administration, women held three of the top six posts on this committee, serving as deputy president, secretary, and deputy secretary, while men served as president, treasurer, and deputy treasurer. The three women elected to the top posts on the Drinking Water Committee headed their households. Two of the women were widows and the third was an unmarried woman who lived with her widowed mother. Three women were also elected to the committee's 12 auxiliary posts.

In 2002, I conducted unstructured interviews with 21 residents (13 men and eight women) who had been or currently were holding a civil or religious cargo. When I asked about the election of women to civil cargos, all 21 respondents felt it was a good idea to have women serving in the delegación and that it has now become part of selecting all civil and religious cargo holders. Respondents also explained that it would not be fair to elect only men to civil cargos because the community was growing rapidly and the roster of eligible households includes many female-headed households. They reiterated the common perspective that each property owner who benefits from piped water and other community resources should be obligated to fulfill cargo obligations. Others justified the election of women to the Drinking Water Committee by noting that women had already held lower posts of the civil–religious hierarchy and were therefore familiar with customary laws and practices that linked water management and cargo service. Respondents noted that the election of women represented a departure from prior practices, and acknowledged that the community might be reluctant at this time to elect women to the highest posts as *delegadas* or as heads of committees. Although a few residents still may oppose electing women, the general consensus elected the slate of civil officers at a community assembly attended by both men and women where nobody openly opposed electing women.

Men and women responded similarly about women's service on the Drinking Water Committee. For example, a man who was serving in the delegación said, "Women have their ideas as well, so it is good to include their participation. Each household should participate in the delegación." A former civil cargo holder said, "Women have property and interests similar to those of men," and another said, "It is fine that women express opinions in community assemblies, but they also have to work." Likewise, a woman serving on the Drinking Water Committee said, "Because elections go according to a roster of all households and I am a widow, what can you do?" A woman who had previously held a religious cargo said, "We all have our own ideas. Each person thinks differently, so it is good to include women."

Respondents explained that to be elected to the Drinking Water Committee, eligible candidates should understand community customs, be able to read and write, and have other administrative skills related to managing the piped water system. As established residents, many women were considered knowledgeable about community customs and had experience participating in faenas, community assemblies, and religious cargos. Residents also said that women have more education than in prior decades and noted that the women on the Drinking Water Committee included a retired elementary schoolteacher, a former office worker in a government agency, and a health care worker. In this sense, as women gain access to education, the community sees them as more qualified candidates to serve in public office.

As in the case of religious cargos, increasing the number of posts on the Drinking Water Committee also increased women's participation without replacing posts that men typically held. The increase in top posts also allowed more officers to share the burdensome administrative responsibilities. Because both men and women participate on the committee, some tasks could be assigned based on local gender expectations. For example, on particularly busy days, male officers might carry out physically demanding tasks, such as inspecting the water pipes and cutting off household connections, whereas women would stay at the administrative offices to collect water fees. A few women said that they had no option but to carry out the civil cargo because they could not afford to hire a man to carry out the duties of the post. Other individuals commented that women who are retired and widowed often had the time needed to serve in the cargo. None of the 21 respondents expressed the notion that gender should limit service on the Drinking Water Committee and, in fact, some suggested that gender differentiation might be beneficial because women have considerable

Figure 6.10 Women and men talked with a civil officer about fixing a section of water pipes in the colonia. *The women expressed particular concerns about cholera and other diseases if the problems were not addressed. The project was completed, as the municipio provided funds for the new water pipes and the residents in La Purificación's* colonia *provided* faena *labor to dig trenches and lay the pipe.*

experience managing water inside the house, which gives them insights on managing the community's piped water supply.

Despite the emphasis on including everyone in the cargo system, the community members tend to elect established residents, both men and women, to the highest religious and civil positions and thereby ensure that customary laws are enforced. In other words, because locally born women uphold community traditions, they are more likely to occupy higher civil cargos than either men or women who recently moved to the community. In this manner, the interests of men and women from established families converge and reinforce the traditional *usos y costumbres* that emphasize communal resource distribution.

WHAT DOES GENDER MEAN TO WATER MANAGEMENT?

Although men typically control water institutions in Mexico City and in other urban and peri-urban areas of the Valley of Mexico, this chapter shows that women in La Purificación are taking on greater public roles in water management even though gender differentiation limited their participation in prior decades. Women's growing participation is tied to economic and social changes that give women access to wage jobs and education, and allow them to become heads of households. Although women's status is changing, both men and women often comment that women's participation in local water management makes sense because of, and not despite, traditional gender norms and expectations. In other words, traditional culture intensifies women's participation rather than holds them back. Women are extending their traditional roles as managers of water in the household to community water management. The fact that most of the women elected to civil cargos for the first time were assigned to the Drinking Water Committee rather than chosen as heads of the delegación or as members of other administrative committees illustrates this role extension.

Though it is new to see women elected as public water officials in Mexico, my analysis resonates with other accounts of women's grassroots efforts in Latin America where women expand rather than abandon their traditional roles as wives, mothers, and daughters (Bennett 1995a, 1995b; Bennett et al. 2005; Elmendorf 1981; Flores 1995; García Lascuráin 1995; Jelín 1990; Safa 1990; Tortajada 2000). Such studies show that, particularly during economic downturns, women's participation in resource distribution helps counter market-based forces that favor wealthier individuals and groups. As the Mexican state seeks to privatize water management, women and men in La Purificación participate in local efforts to maintain community-based water management systems rather than to allow the municipio or private companies to manage limited water supplies as a commodified service (for more on privatization issues, see Ennis-McMillan 2002). Women's ideas, experiences, and leadership are valued contributions to an effective bottom-up water management approach that emphasizes participation, equity, and cooperation rather than the top-down economic policies that promote competition, commodification, and exclusion.

At the same time that women in La Purificación reinforce and extend traditional gender expectations, their involvement in water issues signals a transformation of women's traditional gender roles. In part, this change relates to the importance placed on a system that is level or parejo, which implies that all households should participate in a community-based form of water management. Women are listed in significant numbers as piped water consumers and provide crucial money, time, and labor for operating the water system. Women's increasing participation in water management is supported by better access to formal education and wage work and their subsequent ability to purchase property. In contrast to the situation reported for urban women in the Valley of Mexico, women in this foothill community have access to local water institutions and, for the moment, are able to use avenues of action other than protest to address their grievances over water issues (see Bennett 1995a, 1995b; Flores 1995; García Lascuráin 1995).

The ethnographic information in this chapter also shows how gender intersects with class and residency status, because men and women from established families with ties to agriculture hold the most authority over the administration of local water supplies, and obligate newcomers to participate in community customs to maintain household water connections. This former campesino community has limited any attempts by newcomers and outside entities to institute a water distribution system that would tend to channel water to households of higher socioeconomic strata as occurs in other areas of the Valley of Mexico. In La Purificación, women use their new positions of authority to influence the course of community development, and they help create and enforce local non-market policies that regulate access to and distribution of limited water supplies. By linking private interests in household water with the public water administration, women have been able to exercise and acquire a certain measure of power. As the women in La Purificación show us, their management of water is often at the center of the life of any pueblo.

7/"We are Suffering from Water"
Health and Resource Scarcity

"Estamos sufriendo del agua" (we are suffering from water) is a phrase I often heard during my research in La Purificación. Previous chapters explored how los Purifiqueños engage in a variety of individual and collective struggles to obtain water for drinking and other basic necessities. In this chapter, I use a medical anthropology perspective to examine how los Purifiqueños link their suffering to unhealthy water quality, quantity, and distribution. Although los Purifiqueños are concerned about unhealthy water quality, they experience periods when they are equally if not more concerned about the pain and anxiety associated with water scarcity and improper distribution. Residents talk about water-related suffering in ways that do not correspond to biomedical categories of illness but that reveal the physical, emotional, and social hardships they experience with inadequate household water supplies. This ethnographic analysis focuses particularly on how los Purifiqueños discuss "suffering from water" as part of their effort to deal with the social dimensions of water scarcity. This part of the case study challenges us to think about water-related health issues more broadly than biomedical concerns for water quality.

DON'T DRINK THE WATER?

At a convenience store not far from my home in Saratoga Springs, New York, I ran into Nick, one of my former students. We chatted for a moment. Nick had just graduated from college and was working in town for the summer before moving out west. He asked me about my summer plans, and I told him I was going back to Mexico to do some summer research.

As I set my coffee on the counter, the cashier asked, "You are going to Mexico?"

I said, "Yes."

"Well," she said with a smile and a cheerful voice, "Don't drink the water." She laughed.

I quickly glanced at Nick who had a knowing grin on his face. He had been in my class and heard me discuss my water research in Mexico. He knew that water-related health issues were complex and went beyond U.S. preoccupations with water quality.

The cashier looked puzzled and said, "I heard you aren't supposed to drink the water in Mexico. You can get sick."

I told her that I had heard this idea many times and assured her that I would be careful. I paid for my coffee, wished Nick good luck, and headed back to my office at the college.

This sort of exchange has become a routine part of my traveling to Mexico. I commonly hear "don't drink the water" and other comments about unclean water, Montezuma's revenge, and diarrhea whenever I prepare to leave the United States for Mexico. Friends and acquaintances always seem surprised that I did not get sick from drinking the water while living in a rural Mexican community. I, on the other hand, am always surprised that people are preoccupied with Mexico's water quality.

While living in La Purificación, I did take all the usual precautions recommended to travelers in Mexico. I regularly purified drinking water by boiling it or adding bleach to it. I cooked with purified water and even brushed my teeth with purified water. I drank bottled water when it was an option outside of the house, but when visiting families, I could not guarantee that the water had been purified.

Even in the family with whom I lived, I could not be sure the water was purified in ways that would be acceptable to most people in the United States. During my first summer in La Purificación, I typically ate at least one meal a day with Amelia and her mother Sarita. We usually had some form of soda, hot coffee, or

Figure 7.1 Enjoying a family meal. In this picture, everyone is drinking glasses of water flavored with fruit juice and sugar.

hot tea with the meal. One day, Amelia offered me a glass of water flavored with some juice of the *tejocote* fruit. The flavored water sounded delicious and refreshing, but I asked if she had boiled the water. She assured me she had.

I asked Amelia, "How long did you boil the water?"

She replied, "For a little bit." It turns out she had heated the water until it was hot, but did not bring it to a full boil. I knew that at the high altitude it took a relatively long time to boil the water.

"Well," I said, "the World Health Organization recommends boiling water for several minutes to purify the water."

Amelia gasped. She said she knew people boiled water for a long time. She said, "But that would waste a lot of gas."

I replied, "It's better to waste a little gas than to 'waste' a white guy!"

Amelia and Sarita burst out laughing at my play on words. Both women told me not to worry about drinking the water. La Purificación's water was pure and everyone in the pueblo drinks water directly from the tap. I cheerfully but cautiously drank my glass of "boiled" water. I did not get sick.

Amelia repeated this story to others. Even years later, each time I visit, she delights in recalling the story about almost "wasting" the white guy.

This story illustrates a general tendency for los Purifiqueños to regard their piped water supply as clean and safe for drinking. The Drinking Water Committee has no routine formal mechanisms for monitoring or controlling the quality of the piped water. Households informally monitor the quality of both surface water and groundwater by looking at and smelling the water. It is up to individual households to purify their water. In contrast to most Americans, los Purifiqueños have relatively few concerns about drinking the water.

LOCAL PERCEPTIONS OF WATER QUALITY

When talking about suffering from water, residents did not associate suffering with compromised water quality. They based their views of drinking water quality on their health, which they perceive as good, and on the physical qualities of the water, such as its color, smell, and taste. Community residents suggest, for example, that the community's drinking water supply is relatively clean (*limpia*), pure (*pura*), and healthy (*sana*), especially when compared to polluted surface water from irrigation ditches and treated water from water trucks. Residents note that the water looks pure and lacks visible signs of pollution.

In interviews, nobody reported that they or a family member had become sick from the drinking water. As one woman told me, "We have never had an epidemic." In 1996, I interviewed 41 residents who at that time were or had been *cargo* holders. None of the interviewees reported that they purified their drinking water before consuming it, and only two of the 41 individuals reported that they boiled or filtered water before drinking it. Because these residents directly managed the water and had extensive knowledge about the water supply, I assumed that the data reflected a general tendency of most residents. In conversations, people commonly pointed out that they probably should purify their drinking water according to national health education messages about cholera and diarrheal diseases that they had heard on television and radio. At meals, residents often joked about foreigners like myself wanting *agua purificada* (purified water), which, they pointed out, was readily available because the community was called La Purificación.

Some local civil officials, however, have become concerned about the quality of the drinking water especially after directly observing how water travels through the piped system. Members of the Drinking Water Committee have found water pipes plugged with garbage, pieces of cloth, leaves, sticks, and dead animal parts. Officials also have become concerned while cleaning the piped water system. Once a year on Easter Saturday (Sábado de Gloria), local officials coordinate an annual *faena* to clean the system. On that morning, they shut off the entire system and clean the water tanks. A group of neighbors clean each tank with bleach and brooms and allow the bleached water to flush through the whole system. Other than this day, not much is done to clean the water system and chlorine is not added to the water.

The Municipio of Texcoco has carried out biochemical water tests for La Purificación and other communities. Water quality tests that the National Polytechnic Institute in Mexico City conducted in 1992 examined the water in terms of standards recommended by Mexico's Secretary of Health and tested for the hardness, pH, alkalinity, detergents, aerobic organisms, coliform bacteria, and suspended solids. In La Purificación, samples were taken of the groundwater from the piped water system and the surface water used for irrigation. In

Figure 7.2 Cleaning the community water tanks, an annual event that takes place on Easter Saturday (Sábado de Gloria). In this picture, young men and boys splash each other with water and laugh while cleaning the tank.

addition, a control sample from the drinking water system of Texcoco was taken to compare with La Purificación's samples. The report concluded that, "according to the microbial analysis, the drinking water samples from Texcoco meet the established norms of the Secretary of Health and the water is acceptable for human consumption. The other water samples do not comply with the norms and are not acceptable for human consumption." In particular, the test results show that the community's groundwater and surface water did not meet public health standards regarding levels of *E. coli* and other disease-causing microorganisms that originate from human and animal fecal matter. Samples from the well and the first water tank did not exceed acceptable levels of disease-causing coliform bacteria, but samples from two of the three large water tanks and the irrigation water exceeded acceptable levels of coliform bacteria.

These findings support statements by authorities in La Purificación who said that groundwater directly from the well is a clean water source. The biochemical data indicate that after leaving the main well, water in pipes, water tanks, and household faucets becomes polluted with disease-causing microbes, something that is not generally recognized in the community. The water probably becomes polluted as it travels through the system, which is not self-contained.

The large water tanks have openings, and many household connections have pipes and rubber hoses that leak water and are surrounded by impurities that can enter the system. This problem is compounded by the fact that many pipes and hoses for domestic water run inside irrigation canals in areas where the rocky terrain makes it difficult to dig trenches for laying water pipes. Many households discharge gray water and sewage water onto their gardens, irrigation canals, and streets. Household water pipes and hoses that run above ground are exposed to this wastewater, which allows pollutants to enter the piped water system. Because officials turn the water pump on for a few hours a day, the system does not have positive pressure 24 hours a day. Turning the pump off creates negative pressure that draws impurities into openings in the water system. Based on these data and other reports, physicians and public health workers in the region suggest that the water supplies of La Purificación and nearby communities put residents at risk for parasitic diseases and cholera.

WHAT IS SUFFERING FROM WATER?

Despite the health risks associated with water quality, community residents value having a relatively clean source of water that can be used for drinking as well as cooking, bathing, laundry, and other basic necessities. Not only is the piped water cleaner than surface water used for irrigation, but it is delivered in greater amounts and in a more reliable manner. From the perspective of local residents, the major water issues are not confined to water quality. Rather, the major issues involve dealing with suffering from inadequate water supplies for daily needs. During water shortages, residents complain about suffering from water when they have no water for drinking, let alone for household chores.

"Suffering from water" is a common local idiom in the community life in La Purificación, something that I heard repeatedly while visiting households, walking in the streets, and participating in public events and activities. For residents, phrases such as *sufrir del agua* (to suffer from water) and *sufriendo del agua* (suffering from water) refer to an aspect of community life that is so routine and prevalent it requires little explanation. When I began explicitly eliciting comments on the meaning of the phrase "suffering from water," my questions surprised residents. For example, when I visited Carmen and shared the midday meal with her family, she described to those gathered around the table some interview questions I had asked her a few days earlier. Laughing, she said that I had asked her the meaning of the phrase "to suffer from water." Carmen asked her family, in a tone that was part mocking and part disbelief, "Can you believe that he doesn't know what that means?" Similarly, when I asked Amelia about the phrase "suffering from water," she shook her head, laughed, and said that I would not know because I had probably never suffered from water. Most striking, perhaps, was that los Purifiqueños used the local idiom "we are suffering from water" to express a collective bodily distress due to persistent water scarcity.

During the interview when I asked Carmen about the meaning of the phrase "suffering from water," she responded by saying,

> We suffer from having to struggle and having to run around paying for water from water trucks, or when we don't have sufficient water for our necessities . . . like for bathing, for washing clothes . . . . This is suffering, because, [during the last water shortage], just like before [the community had a piped water system], we have to carry clothes over to the river by Molino de Flores, our clothes. I have a little car, and I take [laundry] in the car, and we wash over there [at the river]. All of this we call suffering from water, because we don't have our water in the house, no water to fill buckets, not enough water even to bathe each week, so for me this is a terrible suffering . . . carrying our water in pots and buckets. And when I want to bathe, really it is draining, how one suffers. . . .

These types of statements reflect the social aspects of the residents' suffering from lack of adequate water.

During my observations in the civil offices, I heard community residents discuss their suffering with water authorities. In an interview, I asked Carlos, the president of the Drinking Water Committee, what residents meant when they said they were suffering from water, and he explained:

> I can suffer in the sense that I don't have the service for the most indispensable things . . . such as for preparing the food and for, well, for drinking. For bathing, if you have irrigation water, well you can use that. And one suffers about their allotted supply not arriving, that amount requested of, let's say, 13 gallons per person, and it doesn't arrive. We have seen families with five people who are supplied with a metal drum of 53 gallons every other day. Now, with the amount, it would be about 10 gallons per person [every other day], no? But, it would be half, 5 gallons, daily, while other people have double or triple or more. This would be suffering, to not have water and being obligated to pay for it, you know, hoping that the water will arrive. . . . [Then] this would be suffering, more than anything, moral [suffering], to see that [my neighbor] has it and I don't have it.[1]

---

[1] I converted liters to gallons to keep the units consistent throughout the text.

Figure 7.3 Interviewing Carmen. I tape-recorded the interview and used an open-ended questionnaire to elicit information.

Like Carmen and Carlos, many residents in La Purificación explained how they and their families suffered when they had inadequate water supplies for daily needs. The preceding comments about suffering from water are similar to those I heard from established residents holding local offices and occupying the lower and middle socioeconomic strata of the community. During my interviews and observations of public encounters, I often heard residents complain that they had little water, sometimes less than 13 gallons per person per day. Residents talk about suffering from water and suffering about water when they have to wait for the arrival of water, ration the use of water in the household, carry and store water, pay for water, and contribute limited time, money, and physical labor to community water projects. Los Purifiqueños also describe the bodily discomfort they and their family members feel when they cannot bathe for days, cannot wash dirty clothes, dishes, and toilets. They speak of their suffering when carrying laundry to wash in a river and when they have to pester neighbors, friends, and kin with requests for water.

Every household expects to receive piped water for two to four hours every other morning. Residents coordinate daily routines around the water schedule and often wait for the water to reach their houses before doing laundry and other activities. When they do not receive adequate water supplies, residents complain to the local water authorities, who are often neighbors, friends, or kin that they are "suffering from water." They demand to know whether it is a temporary technical problem or a social injustice that has prevented them from receiving their fair share of drinking water. As mentioned in earlier chapters, the mountainous terrain and the aging equipment sometimes produce technical problems:

gravity pulls water to households at lower elevations; the water pump breaks down; the electricity goes out; and water pipes and hoses break and get plugged. Residents know, however, that water problems also originate from the social world: residents intentionally tamper with water valves and pipes; households at lower elevations leave water faucets open to fill large water tanks; wealthier households pump water to use in ornamental and commercial gardening; and civil authorities change the water schedule to favor particular areas of the community. Community members especially want to know whether water is fairly distributed regardless of socioeconomic level.

Residents with inadequate water say they are suffering when they see others with more water and using drinking water to wash cars, water lawns, clean sidewalks, and engage in other self-indulgent activities. Community residents who see others with more water describe their bodily distress with terms such as frustration (*frustración*), anguish (*angustia*), bother (*molestia*), worry (*preocupación*), and anger (*coraje*). To them, it is unjust to receive inadequate amounts of water, pay the same monthly water fees, and fulfill the same annual labor obligations as other community members who receive greater amounts of water.

I heard both men and women express this sort of suffering, but my notes include more women voicing such views. During community meetings, for example, women were the majority who spoke up. In fact, it was at the urging of several women at an emergency community assembly that civil officials organized a water commission to make door-to-door requests for contributions for the water system. Women also express their concerns in the offices of the civil authorities, as well as in houses and in the streets during informal gatherings

Figure 7.4 A community assembly about drinking water issues, in which men and women participate.

with other residents. Women explain that ultimately they have the responsibility for water reaching their households, and they take action by voicing the suffering of their families to local authorities when it does not (see Chapter 6). Those from households of the lower socioeconomic strata seem especially vocal about pointing out that they do not have the means to store large quantities of water and cannot afford to pay trucks to deliver water to their houses.

Local discussions about the physical and moral aspects of suffering from water scarcity motivate los Purifiqueños to identify and confront the injustice of that suffering. When the disruption in water supply is due to technical problems, residents pressure authorities to address the issues as quickly as possible, but they are somewhat tolerant of problems associated with the ongoing process of developing a piped water system. Los Purifiqueños tolerate a certain degree of suffering from water if everyone in the community experiences similar burdens associated with scarce water supplies. On the other hand, when water scarcity has a social origin, residents see this as a violation of the principle that residents who fulfill their community obligations can expect to receive a fair share of piped water. In other words, when some residents suffer more than others, they identify this as an injustice. When this is the case, residents are less understanding of any disruption in their water supply and take individual and collective action to address the problem.

SUFFERING AND SOCIAL INEQUALITY

All community members are aware of and concerned about water scarcity in their community and many articulate suffering as a collective experience by noting that "*we* are suffering from water." Nonetheless, the propensity for talking about collective suffering from water depends somewhat on the speaker's socioeconomic position. Most residents of the upper socioeconomic stratum live in large houses with large cisterns that allow them to weather temporary disruptions in water supply. I rarely heard them use the idiom "suffering from water." One such resident had not heard the phrase and another dismissed it as simply improper grammar. Most of the established residents occupy middle and lower strata and hold local religious and civil cargos. Residents from these strata use this idiom as they lead community meetings, meet in civil offices, and go door to door to deal with water debts. In interviews, 25 individuals from the middle stratum and 10 individuals from the lower stratum said they had heard of the phrase and explained its meaning to me. In addition, I regularly heard residents mention in civil offices and community meetings that they were suffering from water because they did not have large cisterns and depended on receiving daily supplies of water. For them, this phrase was a matter of experience and not improper grammar.

The phrase *sufriendo del agua* raises an interesting linguistic issue. Speakers of standard Spanish would tend to use the preposition *por* in the phrase *sufriendo por el agua*. The preposition *por* indicates that someone is suffering because of a situation in which there is no water and implies a measure of agency and volition on the part of the sufferer. In other words, *por* signals that the sufferer is the source of the action (that is, the suffering) in relation to a particular situation at a particular time, such as what would result from an occasional disruption in the water supply. This grammatical structure also implies that the situation could be resolved with a simple intervention. By contrast, los Purifiqueños use the preposition *de* in the phrase *sufriendo del agua*. This phrase would tend to sound nonstandard and ungrammatical to many speakers of Spanish, which some residents suggested. Nevertheless, the preposition *de* signals that the water has a certain measure of agency in causing the suffering and that the suffering is related to a situation that has an ongoing or chronic quality much like an endemic disease. For example, the use of *de* in the phrase *sufriendo de cancer* (suffering from cancer) localizes cancer as the source of the suffering and implies that the sufferer has a limited ability to change the source of a chronic problem. Likewise, the use of *de* in the phrase *sufriendo del agua* implies that water is the source of the suffering and that water-related suffering is habitually prevalent and not easily solvable, if at all.

A person's residency status also influences the experiences of suffering. I observed ongoing conflicts and negotiations between established residents and new residents over drinking water. In public encounters, established residents often state that they, as a community, are suffering from water and that they need to remain united as a community to address water problems. In these discussions, the established residents reminded listeners, especially new residents, that before the 1970s, La Purificación was a poor peasant community. Established residents note that new residents in the higher socioeconomic strata abuse their community privileges by not contributing money or labor to community water projects. They complain that the settlement of new residents places more demands on the water system, especially when new wealthier residents build large houses and ornamental flower gardens. Established male residents contend that in the 1970s they provided unpaid faenas on projects to drill for a cleaner and more reliable local groundwater source.

New residents, on the other hand, point to what they regard as a backward and authoritarian manner in which the established community residents run the drinking water system. Newcomers complain that they pay money for a service that is inefficiently run and not designed properly to deliver water to the neighborhoods where new residents settle. New residents suggest in community meetings that it would be better to pay an outside entity, such as a governmental or private organization, to run the water system.

Established residents generally oppose suggestions to change the community management of the water system and actively maintain control of local water distribution in the hands of the higher civil and religious cargos. They uphold the customary water management practices described in earlier chapters. Because established residents by definition have a longer period of residing in and contributing to the community, they receive use rights to water at lower fees than others who recently settled in the community. Because established residents control the civil and religious cargos, they pass policies that new residents consider controversial. For instance, civil authorities use the support of community assemblies to require new residents, especially those constructing larger houses, to pay substantially higher fees to be hooked up to the community's water system.

"NOT A DROP TO DRINK": RESPONDING
TO A WATER SHORTAGE

Many of the social dimensions of water-related suffering become most apparent during a water shortage. At the end of 1994, los Purifiqueños, like all Mexicans, began dealing with *la situación,* the national economic crisis brought on by the devaluation of the peso and subsequent rapid inflation, wage freezes, and unemployment. Residents regularly referred to these times as "hard," "difficult," and "sad." La situación decreased residents' abilities to pay water fees and complete community service, and it limited the community's ability to obtain materials and pay the electric bills for the water pump. The federal government's new economic policies reduced government subsidies for rural development and other social welfare programs, thereby intensifying the crisis.

In this section, I examine a specific disruption in the local water supply, an instance of acute water scarcity and physical and emotion distress that occurred more than once during my fieldwork. Much of the information related to this particular episode comes from direct observations in the offices of the civil authorities during a two-week period in July 1995 when residents, especially women from the lower and middle socioeconomic strata, told officials repeatedly, "We are suffering from water." Community residents complained that they had no water for cooking, for bathing children before school, or for washing clothes. "We don't even have a drop of water to drink," was a common expression I heard. I examine how los Purifiqueños suffered from water and how they pleaded with their elected water authorities to do something. I found that during the shortage, residents responded by engaging in various sorts of individual and collective actions.

During the period of crisis, the community had no drinking water because the electric company had suspended service to the community's water pump. Officials showed me five unpaid electric bills totaling over 35,000 pesos (about US$5,000). For several years, local authorities had been troubled by the prospect of having to pay higher rates to run the water pump. In 1993, the community discovered that the federal government's privatization measures and the reform of national water laws had ended subsidies for electricity to operate water pumps in rural areas. The reforms in water management were part of Mexico's plans to implement the North American Free Trade Agreement (NAFTA) and other economic liberalization measures. These measures resulted in massive cutbacks in public expenditures for health services, including delivery of drinking water. Furthermore, Mexico had entered an economic crisis at the end of 1994, only a few months after the implementation of NAFTA. In 1995, the electric company increased its rates and the government raised the value-added tax from 10 percent to 15 percent, almost tripling the cost of electricity needed to operate the community's water pump. The decrease in consumers' abilities to pay water fees and the increasing operational costs created a financial crisis for the management of the community's drinking water system.

Consequently, many households in La Purificación had increasing water debts. Using information from the account books of the Drinking Water Committee, I estimated that up to 75 percent of the 844 households with registered connections to the drinking water system had not paid their water fees for at least six months. Many debtors said they understood the need to pay the fees but questioned why authorities pressured them if other households owed water fees dating back to the 1970s. Information from the committee's account books, however, indicated that about 90 percent of the households owed back fees, from between a few months to no more than two years, and fewer than 4 percent of the households owed water debts dating back six years or more. For the community to pay the delinquent electric bills, authorities needed to collect the bulk of the money from the group that owed fees for the months since 1994. During the shortage, when residents complained to authorities at the Drinking Water Committee, authorities regularly showed residents the electric bills as well as the account books for 1994 and 1995. The authorities demonstrated that most households had not paid their drinking water fees and that the current crisis was not simply caused by the few households with long-standing debts.

First Day of the Water Shortage

At the desk of the Drinking Water Committee, I sat, listened, and took notes as Carlos, the committee president, and Pablo, the treasurer, dealt with people who expressed the suffering they endured because of the water shortage. In one of the first cases I heard, a woman of about 70 years approached the desk, sat down, and said she wanted to pay up her drinking water account. The woman said, "There's no water." Carlos explained that two days earlier the electric company had cut the power to the drinking water pump, and as a result, the community would have no water. He said it was a big problem and asked, "How are they going to give us water if we don't pay here?" Other people approached the desk to listen to the conversation. The woman said that many people could not come to the *delegación* to pay their water fees because they worked during the week and arrived home late at night. She suggested that authorities go directly to debtors' houses on Sundays to collect water fees. Carlos responded that they had gone to people's houses, but people never seemed to be home. The woman said she wanted to be up-to-date in paying her water fees but could not pay the full amount that day. She remarked that she had lived in the community for 20 years and had always paid her fees. As he did with many other people during the water shortage, Carlos showed the woman the overdue bills from the electric company. Pablo told the woman that she owed for 12 months in 1994 and 6 months in 1995, a total of 450 pesos. The woman said she could pay only 100 pesos, or 4 months' charges, that day and that she would stop by another day to pay the balance.

Later, another woman, in her sixties, came to pay her water fees. She asked, "If I pay, will there be water or not?" Carlos explained the problem to her and said there was no water in the entire community. The woman asked, in a joking tone, "If I haven't bathed or washed clothes, why am I going to pay?" Carlos responded, "Right now, all of us are suffering." He showed her the bills from the electric company to impress upon her the need for everyone to pay their water fees. Pablo examined her account and told her the amount of her 15-month water debt.

Figure 7.5 A woman confronts the president of the Drinking Water Committee about the lack of piped water after the electricity was disconnected from the community's water pump. Until 2000, only men had sat behind the Drinking Water Committee's desk.

Next, Señora García approached the desk to ask about the water outage. In her seventies, she wore her long dark hair in braids and an apron tied around her waist. She remained standing, arms crossed, glaring at Carlos and Pedro while several bystanders looked on and listened. She had come to pay 50 pesos on her balance, and demanded that the authorities solve the problem. Carlos repeatedly told the woman that everyone was equally affected and that everyone—community authorities and residents—had a responsibility to help resolve the problem. He said, "It is unfortunate that we are now accustomed to the water service, because it is difficult when we don't have it." The woman said it was not fair that everyone whose payments were up-to-date should now be left without water.

She went on to say that the authorities should withhold water from the worst offenders. In response, Carlos complained that neighbors offered little help in locating debtors and that the authorities needed the support of community members to shut off a debtor's drinking water. Because the Mexican constitution considers water to be a national good and guarantees it to all citizens, it is a federal offense for municipal authorities to completely cut off a household's drinking water. In recent years, some communities in the region have organized assemblies and formed larger groups of officials and citizens to cut off water to debtors. As some residents told me, this sort of collective strategy was effective because federal officials would have to arrest an entire community to enforce the law, but this action was something outside authorities have not done and likely would not do.

Señora García also pointed out that some people have private wells and therefore would not have to pay the fees, but that she intended to pay even if her household did not have water. In return, she expected water to be delivered to her household. In response, Carlos eventually pointed out that only a few residents have private wells and that "we are all equals" in suffering from water. The woman simply said she wanted water and handed Carlos 50 pesos. Carlos asked her, "What am I going to do with the 50 pesos you pay me?" implying that more people needed to pay their fees to pay off the large electric bills. She replied that authorities should have warned the community that the water would be shut off. Carlos explained that the electric company had not notified the community that it was cutting off the electricity to the water pump. She asked, "What are we going to do? Have a month without water?"

The morning continued with dozens of similar encounters at the desk of the Drinking Water Committee. Many cases involved residents who owed debts for less than two years and who were outraged that they should be suffering because of the negligence of those with larger water debts. In these encounters, residents came to the delegación to inquire about the source of their suffering and pressure their elected representatives to do something to alleviate that suffering. The representatives often responded that those now angrily complaining would have a chance to deal with these complex issues when their turn came to occupy a delegación cargo and be responsible for managing the drinking water system. Carlos and Pedro assured people that the current officers had not intentionally shut off the water to pressure people to pay their debts. They also tried to persuade residents that responsibility for the problem lies with everyone, as most households had water debts. In this sense, the encounters around the Drinking Water Committee's desk were moments in which los Purifiqueños were confronted by the social nature of the problem before them.

Second Day of the Water Shortage

On the second day of the shortage, I observed dozens of people confronting the water authorities. One encounter between Carlos and Mónica, a single woman in her thirties illustrates the general pattern of the discourse. Mónica, a health care worker, stood at the committee's desk talking to authorities for over half an hour. She said that since moving to the community a few years earlier, she had always paid her entire water fee a full year in advance and yet she had no water. Carlos explained that nobody in La Purificación had drinking water. Mónica asked, "Isn't there another way to pressure people who have not paid?" Carlos replied that representatives could not do anything when the electric company decided to cut the power. He said local civil authorities planned to call an assembly to enlist support for pressuring debtors. Mónica responded that the people who owed would not go to an assembly.

Carlos continued by explaining to Mónica that the local authorities needed support from community members. He noted that in the past when the authorities had threatened to shut off debtors' water, neighbors had not supported the Drinking Water Committee. Also, when authorities had shut off water, people took them to court for disobeying federal laws prohibiting such actions. Carlos stated that although he was willing to shut off a debtor's drinking water, he did not want to be the only person running the risk of being arrested by municipio or federal officials. Carlos said many outsiders with different ways of thinking had moved into the community, and some were opposed to shutting off the drinking water of debtors or of residents who failed to fulfill customary community obligations. Carlos and other officers often reminded residents that municipio officials had jailed previous community officers for shutting off the water to individual households. This threat prompted Carlos to underscore the need for residents to join with officeholders in a collective effort to address water problems.

Carlos continued that some residents, like Mónica, had come to La Purificación from the greater metropolitan area of Mexico City, where they were used to paying much less for their drinking water, and they did not want to pay the higher water fees established in the community. Carlos said he was under the impression that residents of Mexico City had become accustomed to not paying for drinking water and that officials there generally did not shut off the water of debtors. Mónica countered that municipal authorities in Mexico City did regularly shut off debtors' drinking water. Carlos explained that he and other drinking water officials were summoning debtors to the delegación, but, he said, "unfortunately, here there are different customs" and a community assembly had to give authority to the delegación to shut off a household's water. He hoped to have enough community support to mobilize a collective effort to shut off debtors' drinking water. During this and other encounters, Carlos reminded people of the power of collective action to address the social roots of their suffering.

Mónica continued by saying, "I'm not from here, I'm from the district [Mexico City, federal district]." She said that when she bought property in the community, "the *delegados* told me, 'You have to fulfill your obligations with the faenas and the church.' I accepted [these obligations], but now I don't have water and I paid for the water." Mónica insisted that authorities should have been shutting off the water of those who had not paid their bills. Carlos explained that some people wanted him to shut off the water of those who owed for two, three, or six months, but others said people should have more time to pay their debts. For that reason, he needed support from people like her to pass a resolution at the community assembly, authorizing him to shut off residents' water.

Mónica suggested that the authorities needed to explore alternative ways of managing the drinking water system. She said it should be like telephone or electric service, where one paid for the installation and a monthly fee, and if one did not pay, the company cut off the service. Community authorities should be stricter, Mónica insisted. Carlos responded that they had to be careful not to create other problems, for example, by agreeing to "let the government give us state water." Mónica said that government water would be "treated water," which would be worse because "we want potable water not treated water." They were referring to government programs designed to supply rural communities with partially treated and untreated urban wastewater for irrigation in exchange for the right to channel surface water from mountain springs and groundwater from irrigation wells to urban areas in the Valley of

Mexico. These programs are a direct result of the shortage of groundwater in the Valley of Mexico and the federal government's prohibition in the valley against drilling more deep wells for drinking water. Carlos concluded that at least "here, our water, thank God, is very pure, more pure than water they sell in bottles."

Resolving the Crisis

Initially, the office of the Drinking Water Committee was the principal setting in which individuals expressed their suffering to community authorities. After the first few days, residents persuaded the community's civil cargo holders to organize collective efforts to deal with the social aspects of the problem. Focusing on the problem extended beyond the context of the Drinking Water Committee and involved other civil and religious officials and residents. These encounters took place at community assemblies, in the streets, and during large gatherings for baptisms, weddings, and other life-cycle celebrations at residents' homes. Local authorities also put up posters asking residents to pay for their drinking water fees so that the community in turn could pay the electric bill and restore power to the water pump. Officials intensified their efforts to serve notices to debtors, which involved physically carrying summonses to residents' houses. Residents also talked about the problem in settings where they gathered for water. For example, residents hauled laundry to a small spring at the southern edge of the community. Others hauled buckets of water from the spring to their houses. Still others ordered water trucks from Texcoco and paid to fill their household cisterns. All the while, residents complained about the suffering generated by hauling water, looking for water, rationing water, collecting rainwater, and using irrigation water.

Civil cargo holders held emergency assemblies and coordinated a series of collective actions to deal with the situation. During the first assembly, residents accepted a resolution drafted by the Drinking Water Committee stating, among other things, that civil authorities could shut off the water of anyone who owed for more than two months of usage. Residents, however, urged the authorities to use direct means to pressure people who owed payments on their drinking water accounts. During the assembly, several women argued that they needed water immediately to care for family members and said they were not interested in waiting for other residents to pay their bills. At the urging of community residents, the authorities agreed to form a commission to oversee a house-to-house campaign to collect money from debtors. Immediately after the assembly, the first commission sent groups to each of the five barrios in the community. Each group was composed of male civil representatives and male and female volunteers from each barrio (see Figures 7.6 and 7.7). Subsequently, the local male and female religious officials from the barrios joined the commission and helped pressure residents to pay water bills and fulfill community service to keep their water service.

Two weeks after the electricity was shut off, the community had raised enough money to pay a portion of the electric bill. The electric company restored power to the water pump, and the community once again had drinking water.

Figure 7.6 Civil and religious cargo *officers join together to confront residents who have not paid their water fees.*

Nonetheless, to save electricity, authorities further reduced the amount of time that the pump ran. They also continued to pressure residents to pay their water debts. The drinking water commission continued to operate for several months and was mobilized to visit households when an electric bill was due. With pressure from residents and members of the Drinking Water Committee, the commission cut off the water supply to a few households and used them as examples to others who owed water payments. Civil office holders also called a number of additional assemblies to deal with water shortage issues, and each time about 200 residents attended. During each community assembly, residents proposed resolutions and received support, primarily from established residents, to continue to use customary water management policies. The community relied on such policies to address suffering associated with ongoing water scarcity.

CONCLUSION: WATER-RELATED SUFFERING

This chapter ties together many themes from previous chapters and illustrates how individuals and groups experience and express forms of discomfort linked to water scarcity and improper water distribution. The ethnographic details demonstrate the importance of viewing water-related suffering as something that involves more than simply diseases generated by compromised water quality. Individuals and communities also suffer ill health from inadequate water availability as well as the pervasive, daily struggles to secure adequate domestic water supplies. Los Purifiqueños suffer from upset family members, unclean homes, and above all, thirsty, dirty, and aching bodies. Rather than solely pointing to microbes

Figure 7.7 Civil cargo
officers cut off the piped
water connection of a
house with water debts.

in the natural world, people locate the origins of their pain, anxiety, and bodily discomfort in the social world. This medical anthropology perspective of water-related suffering broadens typical views of the hardships associated with water scarcity.

I was especially struck by the collective responses with which people addressed the social aspects of water scarcity. I rarely heard an individual say, "*I* am suffering from water." More often I heard a resident use the expression, "*we* are suffering from water," which pointed to various groups of people with differing interests: families, neighborhoods, poor residents, established residents, rural people, or the entire community. Within the community, poor residents expressed rage at wealthier residents, nondebtors pressured debtors, female residents protested to male water authorities, and established residents resisted attempts by new residents to change communal water management practices. This shows how individuals draw on a shared identity as sufferers facing a common hardship to identify and confront others from outside their particular social groups who pose a threat to the fair distribution of domestic water supplies. With a collective sense of affliction, residents organize group efforts to address the social causes of water-related suffering. In my view, this is a type of alternative healing strategy for dealing with the public health con-sequences of water scarcity. This kind of a strategy shows that drinking water is not simply a health service to be installed in a community. Rather, from a crit-ical medical anthropology approach, water is likely to be a contested resource, and access and distribution must be negotiated and monitored as closely as its quality.

8/Searching for Equity
Critical Reflections
on Emerging Global
Water Issues

An anthropological case study provides a powerful lens through which to better understand emerging global water issues. For some, anthropology acts as a form of cultural critique because it "disrupts common sense and makes us reexamine our taken-for-granted assumptions" (Marcus and Fischer 1986, 1). Living in La Purificación certainly prompted me to question my taken-for-granted assumptions about water, and I wrote this ethnographic account as one way to critically reflect on broader assumptions about the importance of water in daily life. La Purificación faces water problems that many communities around the globe will confront often in coming decades. Like los Purifiqueños, we cannot limit our concerns to water purity, but must also examine how individuals and groups can secure adequate amounts of water to meet basic daily needs and alleviate water-related suffering. Los Purifiqueños challenge us to see that water management is part of a cultural process and can be guided by values of equity, reciprocity, and notions of participatory decision-making.

In this concluding chapter, I return to some of the broader issues raised in Chapter 2, "On the Edge of a Water Crisis." Fresh water is a resource that countries can no longer take for granted, if they ever did. The world's water reserves are under stress, and the international community is searching for new visions of water management to guide efforts for addressing the water crisis. Any new international vision must avoid narrow views of traditional culture as an obstacle to effective water development. I frame this closing chapter by examining the global conversation concerning four water management guidelines, called the Dublin Principles, which resulted from the 1992 Dublin Conference on Water and the Environment (United Nations 1992). Using a *purifiqueña* perspective, I reflect on each principle and explore ways to incorporate anthropological views of water and culture into broader discussions about global water issues.

AN ESSENTIAL RESOURCE

Dublin Principle No. 1—Fresh water is a finite and vulnerable resource,
essential to sustain life, development, and the environment.

Fresh water is a finite resource and one that is becoming less available as the
world's population increases and intensive extraction of water generates water
pollution, water scarcity, and unequal water distribution. Los Purifiqueños live
in a community that reminds each member—even the visiting anthropologist—
not to take drinking water for granted. Indeed, common phrases from community discussions about water regularly echo in my head:

¡Agua es un líquido precioso!	Water is a precious liquid!
¡Agua es el alma del pueblo!	Water is the soul of the pueblo!
¡Agua es un líquido vital!	Water is a vital liquid!
¡Agua es la vida!	Water is life!

Similar expressions can be heard in languages throughout the world, especially
in areas where marginal populations suffer as a result of unnecessary and wasteful overconsumption of water. Have we reached the point where we can hear
such alarms expressed in every language? After hearing more of these concerns,
the international community is considering new water management approaches
that are less threatening to human health and the environment.

To be sure, factors related to engineering, medicine, and environmental sciences affect water management systems. Nevertheless, international development efforts can no longer rely primarily on top-down transfers of engineering
and public health technology or assume that market-based economic principles
should replace supposedly outdated and inefficient traditional forms of water
management. My anthropological case study challenges the all-too-common
misconception that modern water systems should replace tradition to solve
health and environmental problems in developing countries. In medical anthropology and environmental anthropology, research demonstrates that traditional
cultural practices can be incorporated into health and environmental projects
(Baer et al. 2003; Johnston and Donahue 1998; Whiteford and Whiteford 2005).
As I noted in Chapter 2, prevalent modern intensive water practices in industrial
societies threaten our finite and vulnerable water supplies. Given this situation,
water specialists should examine tradition as a potential model for alternative
practices for managing local resources in accordance with socially and environmentally just values.

This case study demonstrates that principles of equity and reciprocity have
been incorporated into existing community water projects. Residents in La
Purificación continuously remind themselves that water is a finite and vulnerable resource. At the moment when residents request to hook up their households
to the community system, they discover that water is a communal resource.
When residents gain access to water, they must provide considerable time,
money, and labor to the community. Thus, being a good community citizen is
part of the process of gaining access to piped water. In other words, negotiating
for the right to piped water is a principal way of establishing a social contract
between citizen and community. We see that in such situations individuals and

Figure 8.1 Sarita (right) with her daughter and grandchildren after a mass during the Corpus Christi fiesta. Sarita has been an active and vocal participant in water issues and regularly comments in public meetings that water is life.

families learn that they cannot view water as an unlimited resource available for the taking in exchange for a minimal amount of money. Furthermore, the system ensures that residents carry out and uphold these practices while residing in the community. Communities like La Purificación use communal principles for managing the piped water system because such principles fit within a broader set of principles, values, and traditions that residents use to orient their lives.

When considering human health dimensions of this first Dublin principle, it is useful to link concerns about water quality with water quantity and water distribution: water pollution, water scarcity, and unequal water distribution are all health issues. Using an integrated water management approach, it would not be acceptable to address one dimension, such as water quality, in isolation from the other two dimensions. Indeed, a narrow concern for water quality may have contributed to the water crisis experienced in many urban areas. How so? When a water development project emphasizes consumption of pure water over considerations of water scarcity and distribution, consumption pressures create incentives for municipalities to seek purer and cleaner water sources. As a notable example, New York City prides itself on providing urban dwellers with clean, pure water. Like Mexico City, New York City must search farther and farther outside of the urban area for cleaner water supplies. This search for pure water has come at the expense of a poor water conservation strategy and the negative impact on rural life and ecosystems outside one of the world's largest cities. The emphasis on clean water encourages unlimited consumption and further stresses existing groundwater and surface water supplies (Goldstein and Izeman 1990, 131–163).

As I noted earlier in the book, international agencies estimate that over a billion people around the world suffer from inadequate drinking water supplies (Gleick 2004; UN/WWAP 2003; WHO/UNICEF 2000; World Water Commission and World Water Council 2000). Children are especially vulnerable to unhealthy water and sanitation. Many of those suffering from water-related illnesses live in marginal areas with little access to sufficient water to meet basic needs. This suffering most often occurs far outside of our industrialized northern countries, which have more abundant water supplies and corresponding overconsumption of water. Water-related suffering, however, can be attributed to a broader range of factors, which include waterborne disease as well as suffering associated with scarce water supplies. Lack of minimal water supplies creates serious health problems. People feel distress when household water supplies fall below the required minimum of 13 gallons per day per person, and it is difficult to obtain 30 to 50 gallons of water per day per person to live a healthy and comfortable life (Gleick 1996). Furthermore, people living with minimal amounts of water feel added distress upon seeing unequal and wasteful water practices in other areas. Los Purifiqueños express this social suffering when they look out onto the Valley of Mexico and see others controlling and wasting precious water resources. Countless communities across the globe experience similar forms of suffering when they struggle to meet basic water needs in societies that allow privileged groups more access to water. Thus, addressing water-related suffering demands that we consider instituting equitable water distribution approaches.

Los Purifiqueños relate their suffering to issues of water quantity rather than solely to water quality. This should not be surprising. Medical anthropology research demonstrates that we cannot attribute human suffering solely to biomedical pathogens (Baer et al. 2003; Farmer 1999, 2003; Harper 2002; Joralemon 1999; Scheper-Hughes 1992). In La Purificación's case, residents feel suffering from distress generated by unequal social conditions. To be sure, los Purifiqueños are interested in obtaining cleaner domestic water supplies, but residents live with a certain measure of water impurity in exchange for securing greater quantities of water. When they do not have enough water, they suffer from water and report pain, anxiety, and exhaustion as they have to haul water, ration water, and constantly deal with water authorities. The suffering of living with limited water supplies motivates people to participate in the laborious process of installing and managing a piped water system.

Community-based water systems address human health issues, but these systems still face challenges when it comes to addressing environmental concerns. Like Mexico's regional and national water development programs, community-based initiatives demonstrate less concern for conserving water for ecosystem needs. National and state programs emphasize water consumption for irrigation and domestic consumption and rarely seem to address providing water for the ecosystem. Community projects focus on meeting basic human needs and improving drinking water and sanitation services, leaving little room to consider channeling scarce water supplies to address environmental needs. La Purificación residents view the piped water system as part of the community's history of irrigation. Residents drain water directly onto private properties, saying this helps maintain the community's relatively lush habitat of fruit trees and vegetable gardens. To date they have resisted efforts to install an urban sewage system that would drain water away from the community and pollute a nearby river. This approach is part of a general pattern of reusing water rather than simply disposing valuable resources. Nevertheless, residents' environmental concerns follow from viewing water as part of a food production process rather than viewing water as necessary for healthy ecosystems.

PARTICIPATION

Dublin Principle No. 2—Water development and management should be based on a participatory approach, involving users, planners, and policy makers at all levels.

La Purificación's case provides a model of water development with an explicit participatory approach among users. This study shows that community participation is essential for sustaining locally managed drinking water systems. For lower-income communities, participation helps lower operation and maintenance costs because users provide labor for water management. In addition, participation reinforces an equitable water distribution system. All water users benefit from the system, and all users must also contribute labor, time, and money to make the system run.

One major way that residents deal with participation issues is to turn to local institutions and practices embodied in the community's *cargo* system. Traditional institutions allow residents to pressure insiders and outsiders and to challenge threats to the continued use of communal water management practices. This study shows how a community mobilizes civil and religious authorities to deploy the collective power necessary to avoid the unequal water distribution routinely found in other areas of the Valley of Mexico. During water shortages, residents consider the less desirable alternatives for obtaining water, such as carrying water from streams, using polluted irrigation water, buying water in urban centers and carrying it home, requesting water trucks, and allowing the government to take over the well in exchange for treated and untreated urban wastewater. Compared to groundwater piped directly to houses, these alternatives would be more costly and burdensome, less abundant, less clean, and, by implication, would generate more suffering. In addition, control over drinking water may be a source of power in rural communities, an issue that deserves further attention in future anthropology research on emerging environmental health issues. Local community authorities who maintain tight control over water distribution may withdraw water as a sanction against those who do not pay water fees as well as those who do not participate in the customary manner. Letting go of local control would risk the loss of the water to others with competing economic and political interests and it would diminish the capacity to shape community participation.

In this case study, one important dimension of a successful participatory approach seems to be linked to the rotation system used for selecting water management officials. Just as water is distributed equitably among all users, the elected positions to manage water are spread throughout the group of users. In highland areas of Latin American countries, rural communities commonly recognize two halves of the settlement and rotate irrigation water across both halves. This form of dual organization influences resource management and distribution. In such systems, the water manager positions are rotated among users from both halves of the community, which balances community authority, obligations, and resources across the community (Gelles 1994, 2000; Guillet 1992; Guillet and Mitchell 1994; Palerm Viqueira 1993). Although this form of water control has been documented more extensively for irrigation systems, communities also adopt similar practices for drinking water systems. This system has a number of benefits, including that it prevents control of water resources becoming concentrated in the hands of a few powerful individuals or in one part of a community. For instance, La Purificación's water officials are selected from both halves of the community (Barrio de Santa Teresa and Barrio de La Concepción), which means some officials come from households located from an area where the water system needs to be developed further. Because water managers are selected from both sides of the community, the distribution system is more responsive to the needs of households in sections that receive poor water service. This traditional form of selecting resource managers might be useful for water development planners, even if it means intentionally creating two halves of a settlement.

Rotating water management prevents one powerful group from dominating exclusive control over the water. Conversely, this rotation system reinforces each user's stake in the system. Users gain knowledge about the system and can participate more fully, either as officials when it is their turn or as informed users when others are in control. Either way, all household members help develop and implement policies that directly affect them. Participants set user fees, determine the volume of water to pump, decide when to ration and conserve water, and determine proper uses of water. Residents also develop citizen-based approaches, such as water commissions, to remind all users of their monetary and labor obligations. Because of the widespread participation, users gain knowledge about how to sustain the system, which includes continuing to reinforce traditional egalitarian principles even as the community updates technical aspects of the water project. In other words, when users control a water system, they have a stake in making sure the resource is distributed properly.

Community participation, however, does not simply emerge from preexisting values of kinship and reciprocity. Politics and power relations form the heart of any participatory approach. I would caution against romanticizing La Purificación and viewing this case as a noble preindustrial community sheltered from the storms of a larger industrial society. Ask los Purifiqueños and they will tell you that participation is hard work! Local language expresses the demands and burdens of participation. One must carry out a *cargo* (obligatory office), complete *faena* (obligatory communal labor), and contribute to and collaborate with the community. Public health programs, including those designed to improve water quality, often attribute community-based program success to effective local administrative, technical, and cultural resources as well as sustained community participation.

Community-based practices emerge out of a history of intense contact with broader economic and political forces, which helps build local resistance to outside attempts to institute intensive water consumption practices. Broader political forces shape local water practices, but often in a negative way. Although rural communities have organized local participation in water management, they have made few direct ties to higher levels of planning and policy making. La Purificación's hidden history of drinking water management illustrates a segmented approach rather than integrated approach to water resources management found in Mexico as well as the United States and other societies. Success at the local level does not always reflect success at higher institutional levels.

For decades, Mexico's central government emphasized development of rural irrigation while neglecting rural drinking water sources. In the Valley of Mexico, small communities like La Purificación built clandestine drinking water projects as they watched the greater metropolitan area of Mexico City quench its thirst by channeling large volumes of water into the city. Whereas water flowed more easily to wealthier households, large industries, and commercial agriculture, poorer groups looked for more burdensome and costly ways to secure basic water supplies. Planners and policymakers turned down rural community requests for drinking water wells, believing that water should be used for commercial agriculture. Eventually, once communities developed their own systems for channeling mountain springwater and groundwater, Mexico City began eyeing these water sources as additional sources for the urban water system. In other areas of the Valley of Mexico, rural communities have exchanged fresh mountain springwater for greater volumes of urban wastewater, which is supposed to provide rural communities with abundant irrigation water for crops. But these programs overlook the fact that the rural communities rely on this same wastewater for household supply, which has created new patterns of water-related diseases and other environmental health concerns (Cifuentes et al. 1995; Cirelli 1996, 2002; Peña 1996). Local participation, including participation aimed at resisting ineffective modern water systems, can protect human health and the environment.

GENDER

Dublin Principle No. 3—Women play a central role in the provision, management, and safeguarding of water.

In rural communities like La Purificación, women are crucial participants in water management. As other water researchers have noted, the third Dublin principle goes beyond saying that women should become more involved in water management. Rather, we should recognize that they already play a central role in water management (Bennett 2005, 2). From an outsider's perspective, it may be easy to ignore women's roles because they may not appear in public as elected water officials. Indeed, with irrigation management, many rural communities recognized men as public officials of the water system. As development programs provided assistance for irrigation development and later drinking water projects in developing countries, engineers and politicians assumed men traditionally took on water management roles.

By contrast, an insider's perspective focuses on women as active participants in a community-based approach to water management. La Purificación may seem unique because women already play a role in water management, something that outsider health and development officials do not always recognize. The community draws on the cargo system to shape women's participation in water management. The local civil–religious cargo system has a flexible and persistent character that has helped the community adjust to the population increases, economic crises, and economic reforms that have affected the Valley of Mexico over the last couple of decades. In contrast to market-based initiatives promoted by government institutions, autonomous community institutions emphasize equity, thereby making it possible for women to participate.

To date, outside officials, programs, and institutions have neither promoted nor opposed increasing women's participation in water management at the community level. Nevertheless, in La Purificación, a community consensus has emerged that recognizes women's contributions to the process of managing a precious community resource. This case study underscores the importance of incorporating a principle of equity—including gender equity—as a way to enhance the sustainability of community-managed water systems. The study also challenges the international community to do better in recognizing women's current contributions to effective water management strategies.

An international focus on women and water brings to light a social dimension of water management that should have been more apparent sooner. Chapter 6 provides the most detailed information about women as water managers in a successful community-based system. Moreover, each chapter incorporates women's perspectives of history, the cargo system, and how communities can alleviate suffering from water. Indeed, La Purificación's case demonstrates that a gender perspective should be incorporated into each Dublin principle. Women demand that others should recognize that water is a finite resource that must be properly cared for. Likewise, women help maintain a sustainable participatory approach and complement rather than compete with men. As we turn to the fourth principle, we see that women also shape economic views of water.

ECONOMICS

Dublin Principle No. 4—Water has an economic value in all its competing
uses and should be recognized as an economic good.

Water is an economic good, but this case study shows that "economic good" should not be conceptualized in a narrow sense to mean "commodity." From an anthropological perspective, economics refers to a group's system for producing, distributing, and consuming goods. For example, hunter-gatherer groups base their economy on wild plants and animals and natural water resources, and then they use egalitarian principles to share the resources among group members. Other small-scale cultures rely on similar economic systems for producing goods from local resources and then distributing those resources among group members. As anthropologists have noted, small-scale cultures tend to base economic practices on meeting basic needs rather than promoting accumulation and overconsumption (Bodley 1996; Lee 2003). Water is an economic good, but cultural views of the economics of water differ.

Anthropologists recognize that large-scale industrial and capitalist economic principles are rooted in a particular and peculiar culture of overconsumption. Rather than searching for equity, corporations seek profit and attempt to control water resources for intensive production of commercial food products and other goods for commercial gain. In an industrial economic system, water becomes a commodity, and centralized governments enforce policies that channel water to powerful groups that use water for economic gain. This dominant form of economic production makes it difficult for many of us living in industrial societies to see water as anything other than a commodity. We live with water bills mailed to our houses and apartments, and we expect to receive this water as a service with guaranteed access 24 hours per day. We live in communities that give discounts to consumers who use more water, and we know that large water utilities manage our aquifers, dams, pumping stations, and water treatment plants. We increasingly avoid drinking the water flowing from our taps, and we buy our water in plastic and glass containers. Our emphasis on a market-based distribution system treats water as if it is an infinite resource ready for consumption to those who have the money. Like most environmental resources, we view water through the lens of a consumption-oriented culture.

La Purificación's case pulls us out of our familiar economic context and allows us to consider the advantages of nonindustrial and noncapitalist water distribution practices and consumption patterns. Within these systems, water is not simply an infinite natural resource. In many communities, individuals and groups work hard to capture water and find appropriate mechanisms for distributing and using the water. In many cases, this involves drawing on kinship, friendship, and other relations of mutual support to provide for basic needs. La Purificación's case strongly reminds us that communities can use alternative economic systems for distributing water. We do not need to think of water as a commodity to be distributed by a market. Noncapitalist systems can provide alternatives to unequal and competitive economic systems.

Indeed, La Purificación's approach to piped water management has noncapitalist features that coexist within a dominant and pervasive capitalist system. The community attempts to restrict access to water rights, not with a market system, but rather based on factors such as kinship, fulfillment of community obligations, residency status, and type of housing. One earns the right to piped water by cooperating with and working for the community. Through the exercise of power and the threat of sanctions, established residents reinforce a sense of cooperation that is related to providing an economically just distribution of piped water. In addition, residents are involved in processes that illustrate the local authorities' productive deployment of power. New residents, especially those of the upper socioeconomic stratum, resist local communal practices, but they also benefit from the tradition-based system by receiving a relatively clean source of water. Furthermore, as new residents participate in local social networks and reciprocal relationships, they accept some of the local communal principles. The system has democratic and egalitarian tendencies such as rotating leadership, citizen participation in policy formation, and fair water distribution. Furthermore, traditional leveling mechanisms, especially the cargo system, reinforce the communal approach to water distribution.

This case shows how traditional leveling mechanisms that distribute water in fair ways can be incorporated into a community-based water system. This process involves continuous negotiations, disputes, debates, and disagreements among users. Residents claim that domestic water supplies, like irrigation water, ought to be managed in a traditional way as a communal resource. Individuals may tolerate limits on the use of a resource like piped water if resource distribution is managed in a fair manner. Residents have been flexible, for example, in creating new cargo offices to manage piped water, and authorities have changed the obligations regarding cargo service. Residents have also created new ways of charging residents for the rights to establish household connections to the piped water system, and they have created new categories of water fees. The community also has developed a mechanism that obligates new residents who did not help install the piped water system to pay higher hookup fees. Further, new types of people are entering into community service, primarily in lower offices of the civil–religious hierarchy, which has given women, new residents, and nonagriculturalists greater access to local authority. Development specialists should examine these features closely in other community-based water projects, because installing piped water is an improvement that may motivate outsiders to settle in a community, which puts population pressures on the water supply and upsets the balance of fairness.

Leveling mechanisms may not prevent social stratification from occurring, but my research shows that they can mitigate undesirable consequences of that stratification. In La Purificación, the cargo system is used to distribute piped water in a just manner, which includes leveling the labor requirements and monetary costs of managing the system and providing piped water to most residents, including residents of lower socioeconomic strata. Analysis of rural communities suggests that the cargo system is flexible and can be mobilized to restrict access to community resources (Collier and Quaratiello 1999; Roseberry 1989; Stephen and Dow 1990; Wolf 1986). My own study provides more evidence of the flexible and dynamic features of cargo systems. In La Purificación and nearby communities, the cargo system tends not to act as a leveling mechanism to distribute productive resources and decrease economic differences, although evidence implies that it may have done so in previous decades. Nevertheless, evidence does suggest that some individuals participate in the cargo system to justify economic differences. For example, wealthier households, especially those of the commercial segment of the upper socioeconomic stratum, hold many of the highest cargo offices and receive access to piped water, which they also use for greenhouse production. Further, economic differences are not leveled because households of upper economic strata occupy cargos less often and use fewer resources and less of their wealth than was the case a few decades earlier, due to population changes and rotating elections. Nevertheless, the rotating cargos maximize participation that leads to an equitable distribution of the community's most valuable resource.

Furthermore, in this traditional community-based approach, drinking water becomes more than a service that people exchange for money according to the quantity consumed. Rather, it is a service that residents receive by abiding by local customary law. Paying water fees is not like paying for other commodities, including from electricity, telephone, and gas companies seeking to make profits. Community-based approaches use progressive fee structures that charge more to wealthier outsiders seeking to move to the former agricultural community. The migrants from urban areas claim that water ought to be an economic good free from traditional cultural practices, but these claims assume water should be viewed solely as a commercial good. Los Purifiqueños suggest an alternative view of water as an economic good within a communal setting. In other words, water is a communal good. This culturally informed economic view of water incorporates a sense of equity and inclusion rather than competition and exclusion.

In La Purificación and other nearby communities in the Valley of Mexico piped water systems contrast with urban systems, which treat piped water as a commodity. New residents, who hold urban views of piped water, often precipitate conflicts, disputes, and negotiations about the meaning of piped water. In resisting outsider views, community authorities maintain tight control over piped water and have shut it off to impose sanctions on those who do not fulfill community customs. In effect, a connection to piped water symbolizes a social bond that individuals have with other residents engaged in activities that have collective benefits. Residents have a right to benefit from community resources—piped water, the church, emergency assistance, and respectable burial sites—as long as those residents also contribute to the community. The community has a stable and just water distribution system because it has adapted to resist outside influences, including the commodification of drinking water.

A market-based water distribution system might seem fair to some observers. Urban systems, for example, rely on valves and meters to regulate and measure water consumption, and, theoretically, people pay according to the amount of water consumed. Water users from urban areas—myself included—might feel uncomfortable with practices that seem coercive. Why should I dig ditches or haul rocks to get my water? What does a religious festival have to do with my water bill? Shouldn't a free-market system allow those with money to be able to obtain better water service?

On the other hand, in the Valley of Mexico, many individuals experience a free-market approach to water as coercive and unjust. Los Purifiqueños live with the contradiction that Mexico's federal constitution guarantees its citizens access to water, but it does not guarantee a fair distribution of that water. Some municipal governments in the metropolitan area of Mexico City subsidize drinking water for wealthy urban neighborhoods and pursue a policy of overutilization of water to supply wealthier areas with large quantities of water. Poor settlements on the outskirts of the metropolitan area of Mexico City pay more for less water

Figure 8.2 An arch over the main road leading out of the community with the message "Have a nice trip."

and spend proportionately more of their household's time, money, and labor to obtain water. That hardly seems fair to those suffering from water. Los Purifiqueños are aware of these issues and the general water crisis in the Valley of Mexico. They know that their social position puts them at risk for losing access to their water supplies. Indeed, they have seen neighboring communities lose control of both irrigation water and domestic water supplies as Texcoco and Mexico City channel water away from rural areas to the urban centers. Current power relations make it difficult for relatively powerless rural communities to maintain abundant water supplies. La Purificación's system with a strong commitment from all members of the community helps them maintain control over their water.

FINAL THOUGHTS: CULTURE MATTERS

The Dublin Principles provide a useful framework for thinking about how to better care for water resources. The principles, however, do not explicitly mention culture, which is a common omission in many international statements on water resources. From an anthropological perspective, culture acts as a resource for mobilizing communities to address a wide range of issues, including, for example, water pricing, local participation, water rationing and conservation, rural versus urban approaches, and the effects of migration on water development. If the Dublin Principles are to guide our future water practices, we should see that each principle depends on viewing human actions in cultural contexts. Culture affects whether we view water as a precious resource, organize participatory water management approaches, understand gender's impact on water issues, and define water as a communal or private economic good. Culture truly matters.

This anthropological research project started with my curiosity about local water practices that appeared unfamiliar with practices in my own culture. Why did los Purifiqueños cut off drinking water to residents who did not support local fiesta traditions? My curiosity about an unfamiliar practice eventually led me to explore a range of issues related to water management and culture in the Valley of Mexico. I lived with los Purifiqueños and suffered from water in ways that I will appreciate for the rest of my life. Indeed, my friends and family from the United States who visited me while I was doing my fieldwork in La Purificación often remarked that more citizens from the United States should have this ethnographic experience to better appreciate water. After living in a community with water running a few hours every other day, I understood the logic behind treating water as a communal resource that required collective efforts. One purpose of anthropology is to make sense out of unfamiliar cultural practices, and Adolfo, Amelia, Sarita, Carmen, and others certainly made their culture of water seem familiar to me. By encountering los Purifiqueños and their humanitarian approach to water, I eventually learned something that should be obvious: water is precious to life.

Glossary of Spanish Terms

The following terms are those used most often in the text and relate to drinking water management in La Purificación. The glossary does not include Spanish terms used a few times and defined in the text, including food items and particular emotions.

agua: water.

agua potable: potable water or drinking water, which may or may not be purified. The term is used in a general sense to refer to water used for domestic purposes. In this book, drinking water is used interchangeably with tap water, domestic water, and piped water.

agua purificada: purified water; drinking water that is purified and considered safe to drink.

agua de riego: irrigation water.

aguador: water carrier. In La Purificación, an *aguador* is an auxiliary officer of the Irrigation Committee and has the main responsibility to oversee the direct distribution of surface water channeled through the irrigation canal system and to individual agricultural plots and reservoirs. This officer also helps maintain and repair the distribution system and monitors the system for ruptures in the canals, damage to valves and gates, and unauthorized water withdrawals. A woman holding this title would be called an *aguadora,* but to date no woman has held this title in La Purificación. (Compare with *fontanero.*)

barrio: a territorial area or district within a community; barrios usually have a name.

campesino: a peasant, which is a rural dweller who makes part of his or her living based on small-scale agricultural production of subsistence crops (in Mexico, the main subsistence crops are corn, beans, and squash). Peasants also rely on other economic activities, such as sale of agricultural produce, wage labor, and craft production, allowing them to pay rent to landlords and satisfy government obligations, including paying taxes. Although peasants live in small agricultural communities and abide by local customs,

they also live in state-organized societies and must abide by government laws. In that sense, peasants are integrated in and dependent on the state.

cargo: a civil or religious office to which people are elected to serve within the local municipal government or the local Catholic church. *Cargos* are usually unpaid, obligatory, elected and rotated among a qualified set of candidates, but some smaller offices are voluntary. In La Purificación, the *cargo* system of obligatory offices follows the definition used to describe *cargo* systems in other areas of Mexico and Guatemala as "a hierarchy of ranked offices which individuals or male–female couples ascend" (Stephen and Dow 1990, 10).

cisterna: cistern, which is a reservoir for storing water, primarily for household use. In La Purificación, most cisterns are concrete, square, several yards in diameter, covered, and underground, and most have the capacity to story 250 to 800 gallons of water. Most cisterns fill with water that comes directly from the piped water system, and many households also channel rainwater into the cisterns.

colonia: a residential district in a community or city. In La Purificación, *colonia* refers to a newer residential district outside of the community nucleus.

delegación: municipal offices in a community.

delegado: a male civil officer who heads the *delegación,* roughly equivalent to a mayor. (No woman has been elected as *delegada* in La Purificación, but women have served in this office in other communities).

ejidataria: a female who possesses a title to a portion of *ejido* land. The land itself is owned by the state.

ejidatario: a male who possesses a title to a portion of *ejido* land. That land itself is owned by the state.

ejido: land held by the community in a collective manner. The land is used for agricultural purposes and was assigned to the community as part of the agrarian reform following the Mexican Revolution. Although individuals possess titles to portions of the land, the state owns the land. The land may or may not include access to irrigation water.

faena: corvée labor, which is obligatory, unpaid community labor usually required of residents in lieu of or in addition to taxes for drinking water projects, irrigation systems, road repair, and other public works projects. Numerous *campesino* communities throughout Mexico require *faena* labor of residents. Residents do the work in a collective manner, so they say they attend *faenas* or fulfill *faena* obligations. (*Tequio* is one of the other terms used in Mexico to refer to corvée labor.)

fiesta: feast day or festival. A fiesta can refer to a feast day to celebrate a religious holiday or a more general festival for a civil celebration or life-cycle ritual.

fiscal: a male head of a *mayordomía.*

fiscala: a female head of a *mayordomía.*

fontanera: a female water worker with the same duties as a *fontanero.* Although women have been elected to this office, women usually pay a man to do the physical work required to monitor the daily distribution of water and help with inspections and repairs.

fontanero: a male water worker. In La Purificación, a *fontanero* is an auxiliary officer of the Drinking Water Committee who is in charge of turning the water pump on and off each day and opening and closing valves to channel water through the municipal drinking water system of pipes and tanks. This officer also monitors the system for leaks and helps install and repair fixtures involved in the distribution of piped water to individual households. (Compare with *aguador.*)

hacienda: a large estate engaged in intensive and commercial agricultural production.

huerta: a small garden for growing vegetables, fruit, flowers, and medicinal plants for household use and for sale in local markets; located in close proximity to the house.

jagüey: a reservoir for storing water, usually for household use. A *jagüey* is usually dug in the ground, round, several yards in diameter, uncovered, and lined with stones and connected to a canal that channels surface water into the reservoir. Most have the capacity to story 500 to 1,000 gallons of water. In La Purificación, most households no longer use a *jagüey* and instead rely on a *cisternas, piletas,* and rooftop tanks for storing water for domestic use.

mayordoma: a female religious officer who helps sponsor and organize annual religious fiestas.

mayordomía: a group of religious officers who organize the annual fiestas for local Catholic saints and virgins. The *mayordomías* are part of the *cargo* system and consist of one or two heads (see *fiscal* and *fiscala*) and several individual officers (see *mayordomo* and *mayordoma*).

mayordomo: a male religious officer who helps sponsor and organize annual religious fiestas.

molino: a mill (such as for grinding wheat into flour), which can be a specific type of an *hacienda.*

municipio: a political unit comparable to a county in the United States. A *municipio* usually has a seat and the territory includes other communities. La Purificación is one of several communities in the Municipio of Texcoco, and the city of Texcoco is the seat of the *municipio.*

Náhuatl: predominant indigenous language of central Mexico. Many of the place names in La Purificación derive from Náhuatl.

parejo: level, even, or fair. In La Purificación, a *parejo* distribution of water refers to an even or fair distribution of water among all users.

pileta: rectangular reservoir for storing water, primarily for household use. In La Purificación, most piletas are concrete, rectangular, several feet in diameter, uncovered, and above ground, and most have the capacity to story 50 to 100 gallons of water. Piletas are used to store water for doing laundry and washing dishes outdoors. Most cisterns fill with water that comes directly from the piped water system.

pueblo: the people or the community.

sufrir del agua: a phrase that translates as "to suffer from water" and refers to the discomfort an individual or group experiences when there is insufficient water to meet basic needs, such as for drinking, bathing, preparing food, washing dishes, and doing laundry.

toma: water connection or outlet.

usos y costumbres: use rights and customs; unwritten customary laws that govern local rights and obligations related to rights to use local resources (for example, water, cemetery plots) and obligations to perform community service (for example, *faena, cargo* service); usually passed on by oral tradition.

References

Alley, Kelly D. 2002. *On the banks of the Ganga: When wastewater meets a sacred river.* Ann Arbor: Univ. of Michigan Press.

———. 1994. Ganga and Gandagi: Interpretations of pollution and waste in Benaras. *Ethnology* 33 (2):127–145.

Baer, Hans, Merrill Singer, and Ida Susser. 2003. *Medical anthropology and the world system.* 2nd ed. Westport, CT: Bergin & Garvey.

Barlow, Maude, and Tony Clark. 2002. *Blue gold: The fight to stop the corporate theft of the world's water.* New York: The New York Press.

Bennett, Vivienne. 2005. Introduction. In *Opposing currents: The politics of water and gender in Latin America,* ed. Vivienne Bennett, Sonia Dávila-Poblete, and María Nieves Rico, 1–9. Pittsburgh, PA: Univ. of Pittsburgh Press.

———. 1995b. Gender, class, and water: Women and the politics of water service in Monterrey, Mexico. *Latin American Perspectives* 22 (2):76–99.

———. 1995a. *The politics of water: Urban protest, gender, and power in Monterrey, Mexico.* Pittsburgh, PA: Univ. of Pittsburgh Press.

Bennett, Vivienne, Sonia Dávila-Poblete, and María Nieves Rico, eds. 2005. *Opposing currents: The politics of water and gender in Latin America.* Pittsburgh, PA: Univ. of Pittsburgh Press.

Berdan, Frances F. 2005. *The Aztecs of Central Mexico: An imperial society.* 2nd ed. Belmont, CA: Wadsworth Thomson Learning.

Bodley, John H. 1996. *Anthropology and contemporary human problems.* 3rd ed. Mountain View, CA: Mayfield Publishing Company.

Bonfil Batalla, Guillermo. 1996. *Mexico Profundo: Reclaiming a civilization* (Translations from Latin America Series). Trans. Philip A. Dennis. Austin: Univ. of Texas Press.

Cancian, Frank. 1992. *The decline of community in Zinacantan: Economy, public life, and social stratification, 1960–1987.* Palo Alto, CA: Stanford Univ. Press.

———. 1990. The Zinacantan *cargo* waiting lists as a reflection of social, political, and economic changes, 1952 to 1987. In *Class, politics, and popular religion in Mexico and Central America,* ed. Lynn Stephen and James Dow, 63–76. Washington, DC: American Anthropological Association.

———. 1965. *Economics and prestige in a Mayan community: The religious cargo system in Zinacantan.* Palo Alto, CA: Stanford Univ. Press.

Chance, John K. 1990. Changes in twentieth-century Mesoamerican cargo systems. In *Class, politics, and popular religion in Mexico and Central America,* ed. Lynn Stephen and James Dow, 27–42. Washington, DC: American Anthropological Association.

Chance, John K., and William B. Taylor. 1985. Cofradías and cargos: An historical perspective on the Mesoamerican civil–religious hierarchy. *American Ethnologist* 12 (1):1–26.

Cifuentes, Enrique, Ursula Blumenthal, and Guillermo Ruiz-Palacios. 1995. Riego agrícola con aguas residuales y sus efectos sobre la salud en México. In *Agua, Salud y Derechos Humanos,* ed. Iván Restrepo, 189–201. Mexico, DF: Comisión Nacional de Derechos Humanos.

Cirelli, Claudia. 2002. Supplying water to the cities: Mexico City's thirst and rural water rights. In *Protecting a sacred gift: Water and social change in Mexico,* ed. Scott Whiteford and Roberto Melville, 151–161. La Jolla: Center for U.S.–Mexican Studies, University of California, San Diego.

———. 1996. Abasto de agua a las ciudades: la perspectiva de las zonas abastecedoras—el caso de San Felipe y Santiago, Alto Lerma. In *Apropriación y usos del* agua: nuevas líneas de investigación, eds. Roberto Melville and Francisco Peña, 65–80. Estado de México: Universidad Autónoma Chapingo.

Collier, George A., and Elizabeth Lowery Quaratiello. 1999. *Basta!: Land and the Zapatista rebellion in Chiapas.* Rev. ed. Oakland, CA: Food First Books.

CountryWatch. 2005. Mexico. People. http://www.countrywatch.com (accessed August 14, 2005).

Cox, Stephen, and Sheldon Annis. 1988. Community participation in rural water supply. In *Direct to the poor: Grassroots development in Latin America,* ed. Sheldon Annis and P. Hakim, 65–72. Boulder, CO: Lynne Rienner Publishers.

DeVilliers, Marq. 2001.*Water: The fate of our most precious resource.* Boston, MA: Houghton Mifflin.

———. 1999. *Water wars: Is the world's water running out?* London: Weidenfield and Nicolson.

DeWalt, Billie R. 1975. Changes in the cargo system of Mesoamerica. *Anthropological Quarterly* 48 (2):87–105.

Doolittle, William E. 1990. *Canal irrigation in prehistoric Mexico: The sequence of technological change.* Austin: Univ. of Texas Press.

Elmendorf, Mary. 1981. *Women, water and the decade.* Water and Sanitation for Health Project, Technical Report 6 (OTD 35). Washington, DC: Agency for International Development.

Enge, Kjell I., and Scott Whiteford. 1989. *The keepers of water and earth: Mexican rural social organization and irrigation.* Austin: Univ. of Texas Press.

Ennis-McMillan, Michael C. 2005. La vida del Pueblo: Women and household water management in the Valley of Mexico. In *Opposing currents: The politics of water and gender in Latin America,* ed. Vivienne Bennett, Sonia Dávila-Poblete, and María Nieves Rico, 137–153. Pittsburgh, PA: Univ. of Pittsburgh Press.

———. 2002. A paradoxical privatization: Challenges to community-based water management in the Valley of Mexico. In *Protecting a sacred gift: Water and*

social change in Mexico, ed. Scott Whiteford and Roberto Melville, 27–48. La Jolla: Center for U.S.–Mexican Studies, Univ. of California, San Diego.

———. 2001b. *La Purificación Tepetitla: agua potable y cambio social en el somontano.* Trans. Carmen Viqueira and Andrea Ruiz. Colección Tepetlaostoc, no. 7. Mexico, DF: Universidad Iberoamericana and Archivo Histórico del Agua.

———. 2001a. Suffering from water: Social origins of bodily distress in a Mexican community. *Medical Anthropology Quarterly* 15 (3):368–390.

———. 1998. Drinking water politics in rural Mexico: Negotiating power, justice, and social suffering. PhD diss., Michigan State Univ.

Farmer, Paul. 2003. *Pathologies of power: Health, human rights, and the new war on the poor.* Berkeley: Univ. of California Press.

———. 1999. *Infections and inequalities: The modern plagues.* Updated edition with new preface. Berkeley: Univ. of California Press.

Flores, María de los Angeles. 1995. El abasto y desalojo del agua en la Zona Metropolitana de la Ciudad de México (ZMCM). In *Agua, Salud y Derechos Humanos,* ed. Iván Restrepo, 399–409. Mexico, DF: Comisión Nacional de Derechos Humanos.

García Lascuráin, María. 1995. Calidad de vida y consumo de agua en la periferia metropolitana: del tambo a la llave de agua. In *Agua, Salud y Derechos Humanos,* ed. Iván Restrepo, 123–162. Mexico, DF: Comisión Nacional de Derechos Humanos.

Gelles, Paul H. 2000. *Water and power in Highland Peru: The cultural politics of irrigation and development.* New Brunswick, NJ: Rutgers Univ. Press.

———. 1994. Channels of power, fields of contention: The politics of irrigation and land recovery in an Andean peasant community. In *Irrigation at high altitudes: The social organization of water control systems in the Andes,* ed. William P. Mitchell and David Guillet, 233–273. Washington, DC: American Anthropological Association.

Gleick, Peter H. 2004. *The world's water 2004–2005: The biennial report on freshwater resources.* Washington, DC: Island Press.

———. 2003. Global freshwater resources: Soft-path solutions for the 21st century. *Science* 302, 5650.

———. 2000. The changing water paradigm: A look at twenty-first century water resources development. *Water International* 25 (1):127–138.

———. 1999. The human right to water. *Water Policy* 1 (5):487–503.

———. 1996. Basic water requirements for human activities: Meeting basic needs. *Water International* 21:83–92.

———., ed. 1993. An introduction to global fresh water issues. In *Water in crisis: A guide to the world's fresh water resources,* 3–12. Oxford: Oxford Univ. Press.

Gleick, Peter H., Ashbindu Singh, and Hua Shi. 2001. *Emerging threats to the world's freshwater resources.* A report of the Pacific Institute for Studies in Development, Environment, and Security. Oakland, CA: Pacific Institute.

Gleick Peter H., Gary Wolf, Elizabeth L. Chalecki, and Rachel Reyes. 2002. *The new economy of water: The risks and benefits of globalization and privatization of fresh water.* A report of the Pacific Institute for Studies in Development, Environment, and Security. Oakland, CA: Pacific Institute.

Glennon, Robert. 2002. *Water follies: Ground water pumping and the fate of America's fresh waters.* Washington, DC: Island Press.

Goldstein, Eric A., and Mark A. Izeman. 1990. *The New York environment book: Natural Resources Defense Council.* Washington, DC: Island Press.

Gómez Sahagún, Lucila. 1992. *San Miguel Tlaixpan: Cultivo tradicional de la flor.* Colección Tepetlaostoc, no. 1. Mexico, DF: Universidad Iberoamericana.

Guillet, David. 1992. *Covering ground: Communal water management and the state in the Peruvian Highlands.* Ann Arbor: The Univ. of Michigan Press.

Guillet, David, and William P. Mitchell. 1994. Introduction: High altitude irrigation. In *Irrigation at high altitudes:*

The social organization of water control systems in the Andes, ed. William P. Mitchell and David Guillet, 1–20. Washington, DC: American Anthropological Association.

Harper, Janice. 2002. *Endangered species: Health, illness, and death among Madagascar's people of the forest.* Durham, NC: Carolina Academic Press.

Hundley, Norris, Jr. 2001. *The great thirst: Californians and water history—a history.* Rev. ed. Berkeley: The Univ. of California Press.

Inter-American Development Bank. 1998. *Strategy for integrated water resources management,* no. ENV-125. Washington, DC: Inter-American Development Bank.

Jelín, Elizabeth. 1990. Citizenship and identity: Final reflections. In *Women and social change in Latin America,* ed. Elizabeth Jelín, 184–207. London: Zed Books Ltd.

Johnston, Barbara Rose, and John M. Donahue, eds. 1998. Introduction. In *Water, culture, and power: Local struggles in a global context,* 1–5. Cavelo, CA: Island Press.

Joralemon, Donald. 1999. *Exploring medical anthropology.* Boston: Allyn and Bacon.

Juan, Mercedes, Filiberto Pérez Duarte, and Manuel Aguilar Romo. 1995. El agua, contaminación y efectos sobre la salud. In *Agua, salud y derechos humanos,* ed. Iván Restrepo, 19–34. Mexico, DF: Comisión Nacional de Derechos Humanos.

Kasperson, Jeanne X., Roger E. Kasperson, and B. L. Turner II. 1996. Regions at risk: exploring environmental criticality. *Environment* 38 (10): 4–15, 26–29.

Kirby, Alex. 2004. Water scarcity: A looming crisis? BBC News, October 19, http://news.bbc.co.uk/1/hi/sci/tech/3747724.stm (accessed January 30, 2005).

Kottak, Conrad P. 1999. The new ecological anthropology. *American Anthropologist* 101 (1): 23–35.

Lee, Richard. 2003. *The Dobe Jul'hoansi.* 3rd ed. Belmont, CA: Wadsworth Thomson Learning.

Leyes y Códigos de México. 1994b. *Ley de aguas nacionales (y su reglamento).* 2nd ed. Mexico, DF: Editorial Porrúa, SA.

———.1994a. *Constitución política de los Estados Unidos Mexicanos*. 2nd ed. Mexico, DF: Editorial Porrúa, SA.

Maas, Arthur, and Raymond L. Anderson. 1978. . . . *and the desert shall rejoice: Conflict, growth, and justice in arid environments*. Cambridge, MA: MIT Press.

Marcus, George E., and Michael M. J. Fischer. 1986. *Anthropology as cultural critique: An experimental moment in the human sciences*. Chicago: Univ. of Chicago Press.

Mathews, Holly F. 1985. We are mayordomo: A reinterpretation of women's roles in the Mexican cargo system. *American Ethnologist* 17:285–301.

McAfee, Byron, and R. H. Barlow. 1946. The titles of Tetzcotzinco (Santa María nativitas). *Tlalocan* 2 (2):110–127.

Melville, Roberto. 1996a. Política hidráulica Mexicana: Oportunidades para la investigación. In *Apropriación y usos del agua: nuevas líneas de investigación*, ed. Roberto Melville and Francisco Peña, 17–29. Estado de México: Universidad Autónoma Chapingo.

———. 1996b. El abasto de agua a las grandes ciudades y la agricultura de riego. In *Apropriación y usos del agua: nuevas líneas de investigación*, ed. Roberto Melville and Francisco Peña, 53–64. Estado de México: Universidad Autónoma Chapingo.

Melville, Roberto, and Claudia Cirelli. 2000. Las crisis de agua: sus dimensiones ecológica, cultural y política. *Memoria*, 134 (April), http://www.memoria.com.mx/134/Cirelli/ (accessed January 31, 2005).

Morgan, Lynn M. 1993. *Community participation in health: The politics of primary care in Costa Rica*. Cambridge: Cambridge Univ. Press.

Nations, Marilyn K., and L. A. Rebhun. 1988. Angels with wet wings won't fly: Maternal sentiment in Brazil and the image of neglect. *Culture, Medicine, and Psychiatry* 12:141–200.

Nichter, Mark. 1988. From Aralu to ORS: Sinhalese perceptions of digestion, diarrhea, and dehydration. *Social Science & Medicine* 27 (1):39–52.

———. 1985. Drink boiled water: A cultural analysis of a health education message. *Social Science & Medicine* 21 (6):667–669.

Palerm Viqueira, Jacinta. 1995. Sistemas hidráulicos y organización social: La polémica y los sistemas de riego del Acolhuacan septentrional. *Mexican Studies/Estudios Mexicanos* 11 (2):163–178.

———. 1993. *Santa María Tecuanulco: Floricultores y músicos*. Colección Tepetlaostoc, no. 2. Mexico, DF: Universidad Iberoamericana.

Pan American Health Organization (PAHO). 2001. *Water supply and sanitation: Current status and prospects. Regional report on the evaluation 2000 in the region of the Americas*. Washington, DC: Pan American Health Organization/Division of Health and Environment.

Paul, Benjamin D. 1977. The role of beliefs and customs in sanitation programs. In *Culture, disease, and healing*, ed. David Landy, 233–236. New York: Macmillan.

Peña, Francisco. 1996. Riego agrícola con aguas negras: el caso del Valle del Mezquital, México. In *Apropriación y usos del agua: Nuevas líneas de investigación*, ed. Roberto Melville and Francisco Peña, 93–107. Estado de México: Universidad Autónoma Chapingo.

Postel, Sandra. 1996. *Dividing the waters: Food security, ecosystem health, and the new politics of scarcity*. World Watch Paper 132. Jane A. Peterson, series ed. Washington DC: Worldwatch Institute.

———. 1992. *Last oasis: facing water scarcity*. New York: W. W. Norton & Company.

Reisner, Marc. 1986. *Cadillac desert: The American West and its disappearing water*. New York: Viking.

Restrepo, Iván, ed. 1995. La crisis del agua en México. In *Agua, salud y derechos humanos*, 9–17. Mexico, DF: Comisión Nacional de Derechos Humanos.

Roseberry, William. 1989. *Anthropologies and histories: Essays in culture, history, and political economy*. New Brunswick, NJ: Rutgers Univ. Press.

Safa, Helen I. 1990. Women's social movements in Latin America. *Gender & Society* 4 (3):354–369.

Scheper-Hughes, Nancy. 1992. *Death without weeping: The violence of everyday life in Brazil*. Berkeley: Univ. of California Press.

Shiva, Vandana. 2003. *Water wars: Privatization, pollution, and profit*. Cambridge: South End Press.

Sokolovsky, Jay. 1995. *San Jerónimo Amanalco: un pueblo en transición*. Colección Tepetlaostoc, no. 5. Mexico, DF: Universidad Iberoamericana.

———. 1978. The local roots of community transformation in a Nahuatl Indian village. *Anthropological Quarterly* 51 (3):163–173.

Stephen, Lynn. 1991. *Zapotec women*. Austin: Univ. of Texas Press.

Stephen, Lynn, and James Dow. 1990. Introduction: Popular religion in Mexico and Central America. In *Class, politics, and popular religion in Mexico and Central America* ed. Lynn Stephen and James Dow, 1–24. Washington, DC: American Anthropological Association.

Tax, Sol. 1937. The municipio of the Western Highlands of Guatemala. *American Anthropologist* 39:423–444.

Tortajada, Cecilia, ed. 2000. *Women and water management: The Latin American experience*. Oxford: Oxford Univ. Press.

United Nations (UN). 1992. *The Dublin Statement and report of the conference*. International Conference on Water and the Environment: Development Issues for the Twenty-First Century, Dublin, Ireland, January 26–31. New York: United Nations.

United Nations/World Water Assessment Programme (UN/WWAP). 2003. *The UN world water development report: Water for people, water for life*. New York: United Nations Educational, Scientific and Cultural Organization (UNESCO) and Berghahn Books, http://www.unesco.org/water/wwap/wwdr/table_contents.shtml (accessed January 30, 2005).

Viqueira Landa, Carmen. 1992. Prólogo a la colección (Introd. to) *San Miguel Tlaixpan: Cultivo tradicional de la flor*, by Lucila Gómez Sahagún. Colección Tepetlaostoc, no. 1, 3–4. Mexico, DF: Universidad Iberoamericana.

———. 1990. Los procesos de cambio en el Acolhuacan. Cuadernos de Posgrado en Antropología Social, no. 6. Mexico, DF: Departamento de Ciencias Sociales y Políticas, Universidad Iberoamericana.

Wellin, Edward. 1955. Water boiling in a Peruvian town. In *Health, culture and community: Case studies of public reactions to health programs*, ed. Benjamin D. Paul, 71–103. New York: Russell Sage Foundation.

Westerhoff, Paul. 2000. Overview: Water issues along the U.S.–Mexican border. In *The U.S.–Mexican border environment: Water issues along the U.S.–Mexican border*, ed. Paul Westerhoff, SCERP Monograph Series, no. 2, 1–8. San Diego, CA: Southwest Center for Environmental Research and Policy (SCERP), San Diego State University Press.

Whiteford, Linda M. 1997. The ethnoecology of dengue fever. *Medical Anthropology Quarterly* 11 (2):202–223.

Whiteford, Scott, and Francisco A. Bernal. 1996. Campesinos, water, and the state: Different views of La Transferencia. In *Reforming Mexico's agrarian reform*, ed. Laura Randal, 223–234. Armonk, NY: M. E. Sharpe.

Whiteford, Scott, and Roberto Melville, eds. 2002. *Protecting a sacred gift: Water and social change in Mexico*. La Jolla: Center for U.S.–Mexican Studies, University of California, San Diego.

Whiteford, Linda, and Scott Whiteford, eds. 2005. *Globalization, water, and health: Resource management in times of scarcity*. Santa Fe, NM: School for American Research.

Wolf, Eric R. 1990. Facing power: Old insights, new questions. *American Anthropologist* 92:586–596.

———.1986. Vicissitudes of the closed corporate peasant community. *American Ethnologist* 13:325–329.

———. 1981. Obituary of Angel Palerm Vich. *American Anthropologist* 83:612–615.

———. 1957. Closed corporate peasant communities in Mesoamerica and Central Java. *Southwestern Journal of Anthropology* 13 (1):1–18.

———. 1955. Types of Latin American peasantry: A preliminary discussion. *American Anthropologist* 57:452–471.

Wolf, Eric R., and Angel Palerm. 1955. Irrigation in the Old Acolhua domain, Mexico. *Southwestern Journal of Anthropology* 11:265–281.

World Health Organization and United Nations Children's Fund (WHO/UNICEF). 2000. *Global water supply and sanitation assessment 2000 report.* Geneva: World Health Organization and United Nations Children's Fund, http://www.who.int/water_sanitation_health/monitoring/globalassess/en/ (accessed January 30, 2005).

World Water Commission and World Water Council. 2000. *A water secure world: Vision for water, life, and the environment.* Report submitted to the World Water Council by the World Commission for Water in the 21st Century, February 15, 2000, in preparation for the 2000 World Water Forum in The Hague. Paris: World Water Commission.

Index